DATE DUE

JAN 0 5 2004			
NOV 1 1 2004			

Advertising

Look for these and other books in the Lucent Overview Series:

Advertising

by John Dunn

LUCENT BOOKS

LUCENT *Overview Series*

Lucent Overview Series

Library of Congress Cataloging-in-Publication Data

Dunn, John, 1949–
    Advertising / by John Dunn.
       p. cm. — (Lucent overview series)
    Includes bibliographical references and index.
    Summary: Discusses the functions, goals, and methods of
advertising and examines such issues as targeting the youth market,
political ads, and the right of free speech.
    ISBN 1-56006-182-0 (alk. paper)
    1. Advertising—Juvenile literature. [1. Advertising.] I. Title.
II. Series.
HF5829.D86   1997
659.1—dc20

96–35920
CIP
AC

Copyright © 1997 by Lucent Books, Inc.
P.O. Box 289011, San Diego, CA 92198-9011
Printed in the U.S.A.

Contents

Introduction

ADVERTISING IS AN inescapable part of modern life. It is especially and inextricably woven into the economic fabric of the United States. Most businesses, industries, and firms would flounder without its help. Advertising not only provides an organized way of linking buyers and sellers, it also helps a product, service, or idea to reach more prospective consumers. Furthermore, advertising is persuasive. It entices new customers and reattracts old ones. Successful ads help to generate interest in a product so that a company can profit from the increased demand.

Advertising's functions and goals

Consumers often benefit from advertising. Ads typically provide the public with useful information about the price, quality, and function of a product. Advertising, however, can also accentuate the differences between competing products; inform consumers of corporate or business changes; provide useful information about new research, medical advances, and technological breakthroughs; or warn the public about potential dangers. In addition, advertising lubricates the distribution process, speeding the delivery of goods, services, and ideas that improve the quality of life for millions of people.

Because of its multiple functions, advertising is no longer confined to the world of business. Politicians have made advertising an indispensable tool in conveying their images and ideas. Environmentalists, social activists, and houses of worship advertise. So do charities and countless other groups and organizations around the world.

Although ad campaigns are a useful method of passing on information, the goal of advertising has always been to sell—whether the product is an item, image, or idea. In the hands of an unscrupulous advertiser, however, the information conveyed may be deceptive or false, and reliance on it may be dangerous. Some individuals also use advertising to belittle those they do not like, or to criticize opinions with which they disagree. Negative advertising can interfere with the free flow of ideas; it can destroy reputations; it can stir up the cauldron of prejudice and hate.

Critics argue that with its sophisticated ability to target consumers with persuasive pitches, advertising convinces many Americans to want and buy things they don't need and perhaps would be better off without. Some fear that since advertising now touches virtually every aspect of American culture, even the most cherished and sacred moments of life can be transmuted backdrops for commercial

New York's Times Square is illuminated with billboards advertising services and products ranging from restaurants to electronics. Advertisements are a vital part of the business world, helping to attract new customers and keep old ones loyal.

A billboard protesting a nuclear waste dump site is just one of many signs vying for attention in this California desert town. Not only are billboards useful in marketing products, they can also help bring about awareness of social issues.

transactions. "I call this new culture Adcult," says author and professor James B. Twitchell. "Adcult is there when we blink; it's there when we listen; it's there when we touch; it's even there to be smelled in scent strips when we open a magazine. There is barely an empty space in our culture not already carrying commercial messages." Many believe that this flood of ads greatly alters society by creating a culture in which even traditional institutions such as religion, the family, and political candidates can be marketed. National principles and personal ethics, critics fear, are being pushed aside by a value system based on buying and selling.

Above all, though, advertising is communication. And as the world embraces the Information Age, advertising is destined to increase in volume and to exert still more influence over the generation and distribution of ideas. In the wake of the present flood of ads and infomercials, many Americans are left wondering: Is advertising a bane, a blessing, or both?

1

The Function of Advertising

"THE BUSINESS OF America is business," announced President Calvin Coolidge during the boom years of the mid-1920s. He's still right. Today, business is one of the big engines that drives America's economy. Across the country, millions of men and women own businesses. But ownership is not enough to generate sales. To run a profitable business, producers must find ways of letting consumers know what they're selling. To accomplish this, people advertise.

Today advertising is so vital to economic survival that it has become an industry in itself and reigns as one of the most important businesses in the United States, if not the world. The International Advertising Association estimates that the amount spent by advertisers during 1991 represented $468 for every person in the United States. Altogether, an estimated $130 billion is spent on advertising each year. Eric Clark, author of *The Want Makers* (subtitled *The World of Advertising: How They Make You Buy*), noted that this huge expenditure makes advertising "the largest information budget in the world."

Advertising, for the most part, is a system of communication that conveys information, paid for by a sponsor, about products, ideas, companies, office seekers (political and otherwise), or services. Around the clock, this information reaches the public through a vast assortment of media—billboards, brochures, direct mail, magazines and

newspapers, videos, telemarketing, radio and television broadcasts, and a multitude of other electronic forms.

Media advertising offers many advantages over other promotional approaches to selling such as the use of coupons, discounts, rebates, prizes, and free samples. For one thing, it communicates over a wide area. Some ad campaigns blanket the world. Advertising's top mass media—television and radio—may also lend an aura of impressiveness, or authority, to commercials and that can boost their effectiveness. Also, electronic advertising can repeat messages again and again, thus reinforcing images and ideas in the mind of the consumer. In fact, TV viewers have the opportunity to witness some commercials a dozen times a day.

Advertising has three main goals: to inform, to persuade, and to remind. Though many ads are also entertaining, if not at times artful, the overall mission of retail advertising is to persuade potential buyers to make purchases. As advertising expert David Ogilvy has observed, advertising is "no more and no less than a reasonably efficient way to sell."

Advertisers use a wide array of media to reach consumers. In magazines, for instance, readers may encounter hundreds of ads, depending on the size of the publication.

Standing above the crowd

The most direct way to advertise is to state basic facts about a product: what it is, how much it costs, and where to buy it. Much industrial advertising is done this way. A manufacturer, for example, relies on straightforward, informative ads in trade journals to locate affordable, dependable components. Generally, these materials lack the slick or flashy approaches typical of ads in a fashion magazine.

But in the general retail market, such as grocery stores and malls—where most everyday consumers shop—the situation is quite different. Here, ever increasing numbers of products and companies make it difficult for any one company to stand out above the crowd. In 1975 the typical American grocery store offered about 9,000 articles. Twenty years later, 30,000 items lined the store aisles. Over 30 new products join the marketplace every day, and each has its own way of representing itself. Presently, for example, there are more than 250 different hair care products advertised for sale around the country.

This intense competition forces many advertisers to try hard to enhance "name recognition" for their products. Experienced advertisers know that consumers are more likely to select a brand whose name is familiar to them, even if they don't know much about it.

Sometimes a company tries to highlight its presence in the market by advertising its name and nothing else, on a T-shirt, a billboard, or other medium. For instance, the single word naming a fruit juice company, Tropicana, is often seen during forecasts on the Weather Channel. Designers of

In the typical grocery store, consumers are inundated with a great variety of brands and products. Advertisers strive for "name recognition," hoping familiarity will influence consumers' decisions.

such ad campaigns hope that constant exposure to a brand or product name will breed familiarity and trust among customers, for these conditions often generate sales.

Catchphrases and jingles

Ad makers also use catchy phrases to help remind consumers of their products. Few coffee drinkers can ever forget that the Maxwell House brand is "good to the last drop." And chicken lovers everywhere know which restaurant offers food that is "Finger-lickin' good." One classic TV commercial for Wendy's, the fast-food chain, featured a crabby elderly woman. Upon inspecting the burgers at rival fast-food restaurants and finding them undersized, the actress demanded: "Where's the beef?" For years afterward, this memorable phrase popped into consumers' minds in many contexts, but the source of the line, the Wendy's ad, was sooner or later recalled as well.

Other advertisers may use musical catchphrases or jingles to remind consumers about a product or to present an appealing impression about a company. Jingles have an advantage over catchphrases because advertisers generally can say more about a product in a jingle's longer format. The mnemonic quality of jingles makes them easy to remember. Some cleverly composed jingles stay with consumers for decades, such as this well-known toothpaste jingle from the early days of TV advertising: "You'll wonder where the yellow went / When you brush your teeth with Pepsodent."

Another example of the enduring quality of jingles is illustrated in the following public service announcement, which schoolchildren have recited for years:

> I'm a bobber, yes indeed.
> I know something that you need.
> Be a bobber just like me.
> Wear a life jacket when at sea.

In addition to creative wordplay, advertisers draw from a long list of other reliable attention-getters to attract consumers. Popular music, zany salesmen, cartoon characters, computer-generated graphics, live animals, and celebrities such as movie stars, models, TV personalities, and professional athletes have all been used to promote products. Even politicians such as former governors Anne Richards of Texas and Mario Cuomo of New York have made commercials. Advertisers hope that celebrities not only will grab consumers' attention, but will also impart prestige to the products. Teens, for example, may be more likely to buy sports shoes of a brand that has been endorsed by a professional athlete than a pair with no such spokesperson.

Using celebrity endorsements, however, may have its drawbacks. When controversial political commentator Rush Limbaugh did TV promotional spots for the Florida citrus industry and Pizza Hut, he provoked a strong negative reaction from consumers who disliked him, his views, or both. After vocal Limbaugh opponents threatened to boycott citrus from Florida and meals from Pizza Hut, the controversial ads disappeared.

Image making

Advertisers often refer to the intense competition for recognition as a "battle for the minds" of consumers. Winning this battle is especially hard for those who market common, everyday products such as cornflakes, motor oil, and toothbrushes—items that are essentially the same no matter who manufactures them. That's why many companies turn to advertising agencies to help them create distinctions between themselves and their competition—distinctions that often have nothing to do with the inherent value of the products.

To achieve such product differentiation, ad agencies strive to create images that become associated with a client

Celebrities are often used to help gain popularity for a product or service. Here, tennis star Andre Agassi and model Claudia Schiffer pose for a publicity photo during one of Pepsi's advertising campaigns.

company's name. The idea is to encourage consumers to have positive feelings about the company. In fact, says Barbara Lippert, a one-time senior editor of *Adweek*, a leading trade magazine, "Most commercials only reinforce the name and make you feel good about the company and that's all you can expect them to do." For instance, a Bell South commercial aired during the 1996 Summer Olympics, held in Atlanta, presented positive, upbeat images of the South and smiling Georgians who were portrayed as happily working for the communications company. By showing such positive images, Bell South hoped to make potential customers feel good about both the South as a place for doing business and the company itself.

A form of show biz

Like producers of TV shows, advertisers often use storytelling elements such as suspense and drama to create powerful images. This technique is evident in the many commercials for health care providers portraying tense emergency room scenes that end with successful patient recoveries and reassuring words from the company that makes such happy endings possible.

Not all companies rely on positive images, however. Outrage over social problems seems to be the identifiable image associated with Benetton, an Italian clothing firm well known for its use of controversial print ads like those showing a blood-caked newborn baby and real people grieving over a family member dying of AIDS. These ads and others like them offend many people but also generate strong public support. By drawing attention to the company as well as its ads, these shock tactics drummed up business and helped to establish Benetton as a major worldwide producer of clothing.

Sometimes, advertisers use violence to get noticed. A recent magazine ad depicted a man's hand twisting a woman's head to draw attention to the Breil watch the male model was wearing. The main purpose for using this somewhat jolting scene was nothing less than to grab the attention of customers.

At the opposite end of the scale is another mainstay of advertising—humor. Little Caesar's pizza, for instance, is well known for its funny commercials. One of its most popular TV spots features a young man who experiences a run of good luck. First, he finds a wallet full of money. Then, a woman shouts out a bus window, "I reconsidered. I will marry you!" Next, a small dog jumps into the arms of the actor, who exclaims, "Buddy, you're alive!" And finally, the character in the ad enters a Little Caesar's restaurant and makes the happy discovery that he has a twin brother. Though nothing whatsoever about pizza quality is discussed, the ad effectively associates good things with Little Caesar's pizza.

Like other forms of advertising, though, humor can be a risky way to get a message across. Some research suggests that all too often viewers remember only the comic features of the ad instead of the product or company's name. But even if the product gets lost in the humorous advertisement, ad makers hope that the connection between humor and the company will bolster the company's public image. Comedy also helps viewers identify with the situations depicted in the ads.

Corporate images

Every business, big or small, projects a public image. Deserved or not, it is the popularly held notion of the enterprise as a producer of goods or services of a certain quality, as a fair or exploitative employer, or as a good or bad corporate citizen (one that contributes generously to worthwhile causes, for example, versus one that is seen as a polluter of the environment). Corporate images—the perceptions linked to big companies—build up naturally, over time, but advertisements are routinely used to publicize favorable perceptions and enhance mediocre or bad ones.

Advertising agencies take many different approaches to the task of molding and publicizing corporate images. Some commercials for the Ford Motor Company, for instance, show the company workforce comprised of smiling men and women from different races and ethnic backgrounds. The goals of this ad are to demonstrate that Ford is sensitive to minority issues and that its contented employees are eager to please customers.

Sometimes, though, a company may undertake an ad campaign to counteract unwanted or unwarranted images already held by much of the public. To many people, for example, the mere mention of chemical companies conjures up negative images of belching smokestacks and polluted streams. An attempt to dispel this conception can be seen in an ad for the East Chemical Company that appeared in *Sierra*—a magazine for environmentalists. The ad depicts glorious sunshine bursting through the trees of a beautiful forest. Clearly, the ad's purpose is to give readers a good feeling about the company and to convey the idea of an "environment-friendly" corporation, as opposed to the threat to nature that some might suspect.

The emotional appeal

Though as a rule consumers claim to prefer commercials that are factual, many tend to respond more favorably to advertising based on emotional appeal. Dramatists and novelists have long known that people generally react emotionally to scenes that depict believable characters caught up in interesting situations. Often, in fact, emotion is a more powerful persuader than any amount of factual reporting.

Advertising images with high emotional content have long been used by companies such as Eastman Kodak. For decades, Kodak has presented heartwarming commercials that portray tender and special moments of life—children at play, weddings, graduations, family reunions. These "Kodak moments" are designed to make viewers think favorably about the company and to encourage them to record these special occasions on Kodak film, even though it is virtually the same as other films.

Advertisers make abundant use of emotional appeal to help people identify with a product. As Carole M. Howard, a public relations vice president for the Reader's Digest Association, once told a conference of advertising experts, "Your research taught us [that] people buy more on feelings, hunches and reputation than on facts."

Creating the consumer

Some image-making ads tell more about the consumers a company is targeting than about the company itself. That is, they induce consumers to empathize with the advertised lifestyle and imply that it is within reach through the purchase of the product. For example, many commercials for Budweiser beer feature hard-driving rock music and young, virile men surrounded by adoring pretty women. The ads assume that this lifestyle is appealing to the target audience and suggest that Budweiser beer is part of such a lifestyle.

A totally different consumer image is represented by a TV spot of fashionably dressed men and women who make their exit from a thoroughbred horse auction by

Young, attractive skiers take a break on the slopes with Olympia beer in this advertisement from the 1960s. Throughout advertising's history, beer companies have marketed their products by showing lifestyles that would appeal to their targeted audiences.

slipping into a luxury automobile, a BMW. Here advertisers hope to transmit the impression that owning a BMW will allow people to feel they can enter a world of glamour and upscale living.

Meanwhile, few TV viewers doubt who is being addressed by commercials for weight-loss products. These spots feature overweight people being transformed into beautiful, trim, athletic-looking men and women. Ads like these assume that many in the target audience will want to change something about themselves as a means of improving their current lifestyle—whether it is to become more exciting, more affluent, or more physically fit.

Advertisers often try to influence this change by inducing dissatisfaction in the consumer. That is, they try to present their products or services as necessities that the consumer will feel incomplete without owning or experiencing. Because many people are not easily convinced that they need certain products, advertisers must continually devise methods to persuade the consumer that their specific product is required either to ensure a desired image or to complete a desired task.

2

Advertising Tactics

ONE OF ADVERTISING'S most highly touted powers is the ability to persuade. Using techniques developed over the past four decades, many advertisers try to *motivate* consumers to buy. The most popular way to motivate consumers is to appeal to their desires and needs. British ad executive David Bernstein once observed that almost all successful ads rely on one or all of these nine human characteristics: self-preservation, love for others, self-expression, envy, sloth, lechery, gluttony, pride, and covetousness. For instance, commercials that depict a handsome man giving his beautiful lover a gift of diamonds evoke feelings both of covetousness and love.

Some analysts might add hate, fear, prestige, envy, and sexual attraction to Bernstein's list. Fear, for example, lies at the core of ads designed to persuade people to take out life insurance, or to enroll their troubled teens at mental health clinics. The desire for prestige is evoked with ads for expensive luxury cars.

To get help in learning how to motivate consumers, advertisers have turned to specialists in the social sciences—psychologists, sociologists, anthropologists, and others—who study human behavior. In *The Hidden Persuaders*, a study of advertising published in 1957, author Vance Packard was one of the first to recognize "the large-scale efforts being made, often with impressive success, to channel our unthinking habits, our purchasing decisions, and our thought processes by the use of insights gleaned from psychiatry and the social sciences." Packard noted

Advertisers often rely on sexual images to market their products. In these Samsung ads, a female model caresses a television set (left) while a bare-chested man holds a microwave oven (right).

that because such efforts tend to take place beneath our level of conscious awareness, "the appeals which move us are often, in a sense, 'hidden.'"

Many of these hidden efforts or "depth approaches" rely on the ideas of Vienna-born psychologist Ernest Dichter, often called the father of motivational research. Based on research he conducted in the 1950s, Dichter developed a motivational framework: "[The first step] is to find out why people behave as they do. The second is to prescribe a remedy and to determine how people might be motivated."

Effective advertising, Dichter explained, "manipulates human motivations and desires and develops a need for goods with which the public has at one time been unfamiliar—perhaps even undesirous of purchasing."

Psychological motivation

Advocates of the depth approach believe that by understanding and manipulating images and symbols, advertisers can influence the subconscious working of the human mind. For example, they suggest that an image of a convertible automobile represents freedom to many consumers, while a four-door sedan suggests conservatism. Some advertisers deliberately use symbols in their ads, hoping to arouse consumers on a psychological level, stimulating them to make purchases that may satisfy (at least temporarily) their hidden desires.

This approach was illustrated several decades ago when ready-to-mix cake packets first appeared in stores. Initially the mixes sold poorly. Advertisers were puzzled: Why did consumers snub a timesaving product that was easy to use, requiring only the addition of water in the preparation? Marketing researchers conducted interviews and soon offered an explanation: the ready-to-mix packets caused many homemakers to feel guilty because they hadn't made the cakes from scratch, as their mothers had done in the early years of the century. Armed with this psychological insight, major food companies reformulated the product so that users had to add milk and eggs when preparing the batter. Eggs and milk are ingredients used when baking from scratch. The necessity of adding these items to the mix supposedly worked on a psychological level both to satisfy the women's desire for convenience and to relieve their sense of guilt. Sales of the cake mixes soon went up.

"Subliminal" advertising

Many Americans once believed that use of the depth approach was getting out of hand. Many were especially worried that certain advertisers tried to "brainwash" consumers with "subliminal" advertising techniques. Periodically, news stories claimed that images of hot dogs, popcorn, and soft drinks were projected on movie screens along with the film. Supposedly, these "hidden" images flashed by too quickly to be recorded consciously by viewers but were picked up by the brain at a deeper level of awareness. And there, many suspected, at the "deep" level, consumers were persuaded to rush into the theater lobby to buy refreshments.

Today, however, many researchers are very skeptical about these tales of brainwashing by cinema. In fact, several observers of the advertising industry have doubts about the depth approach altogether. Social critic Ellen Willis writes: "There is no evidence that [advertising] can in itself create a desire. . . . The idea is superstitious: it implies that the . . . [advertiser] is diabolically intelligent (he has learned how to control human souls) and that the media have magic powers."

The need-creating approach remains a tool that intrigues some advertisers. Increasingly, though, ad executives are turning to more modern approaches that are based on statistical data rather than on subjective, hard-to-prove assumptions.

Demographics

In recent years, advertisers have de-emphasized motivational techniques and instead have concentrated on obtaining and using precise factual information about potential customers. Such data have been made available thanks to several new developments. One is a field of research called demographics. Experts in this field specialize in tracking the behavior of various populations within any given geographical location on the basis of census data (vital statistics, number of representatives of each type of person, and distribution in the target population). Enabling demographers to do their work are new computer-driven technologies that process vast data banks containing staggering amounts of personal information about virtually everyone in the country.

Researchers gather and cross-reference the data in countless ways that allow them to categorize potential consumers by occupation, income, living patterns, age, class, and lifestyle. By sorting out where potential consumers live and what their habits and attitudes are, ad agencies have a better idea of how to plan campaigns specially tailored for almost any segment of the population that shares certain traits. For example, the information that New York City women used thirty times as much makeup as those residing in Vermont gave advertisers a helpful way of seeing that their cosmetic advertising dollars were most likely to succeed in New York.

Zeroing in on ethnic and other demographic groups

The ability to zero in on virtually any group in America has enabled advertisers to take a fresh look at some segments of society that were often taken for granted not long ago. Advertisers can no longer assume, as they once did, that the bulk of America's consumers are white middle-class adults having similar tastes, as well as preferences that can be influenced with a broad sweep of advertising. The U.S. population is more ethnically and culturally diverse than it was a half-century ago. In recent decades, the proportion of whites in relation to the general population began to decline. For one thing, the white birth rate dropped. At the same time, immigration, notably from non-European countries, increased. Today, Asian, African, and Hispanic Americans make up 21 percent of all Americans. But if present trends continue this figure could increase to 36 percent by the year 2020. Moreover, minorities are steadily becoming more affluent. By the mid-1990s, spending in the United States by identifiable ethnic groups was generating nearly $600 billion in revenues every year.

To help advertisers cash in on these trends, a specialized field of demographics called "ethnographics" focuses on the living patterns of America's ethnic populations. For instance, knowing that African-American households watch 27 percent more television than do white families and that Asian men do 62 percent of the grocery shopping enables advertisers to pinpoint their marketing efforts more efficiently.

Ethnographics

Ethnographics is becoming so specialized that advertisers have learned how to zero in on the subcultural markets within various minority groups. Not long ago, for example, many marketers would have targeted African Americans as a single socioeconomic group. Such an approach is not valid today, if indeed it ever was. McDonald's TV vignettes of African-American schoolgirls double-dutch jumping in inner-city settings are aimed at black urban dwellers, not suburban middle-class African Americans, for whom different advertising strategies are devised.

Advertisers are also producing ads and commercials designed specifically for a variety of Hispanics, Asians, and other ethnic minorities, sometimes in their native languages. Gail Baker Woods, author of *Advertising and Marketing to the New Majority: A Case Study Approach,* points out that there is "a tremendous immigrant population in many parts of the country. There will be more

Asian-Americans, more African-Americans, more Hispanic Americans that will have money, go to school and are going to need products. There will naturally be more group marketing."

Advertisers are using demographic data to target groups that are differentiated by factors other than race and ethnicity. Having discovered that America's "over-fifty" population has a combined income of $800 billion, for instance, many advertisers are focusing marketing strategies on the growing "gray market." Meanwhile, others are concentrating on once overlooked groups such as handicapped consumers and gay consumers.

Psychographics

Another new field that helps advertisers better understand consumers is "psychographics." According to its founder, Arnold Mitchell, psychographics encompasses

One way advertisers try to reach minority groups is by producing ads and commercials in other languages, like this Coca-Cola billboard that advertises in Spanish.

"the entire constellation of a person's attitudes, beliefs, opinions, hopes, fears, prejudices, needs, desires, and aspirations that, taken together, govern how one behaves."

Unlike the depth approach, psychographics tries to ascertain customer preferences by using surveys and questionnaires to study how people in certain marketing groups actually behave. Such information provides advertisers with "customer profiles" of consumers, which researchers compare, searching for common characteristics that can be exploited for marketing purposes. Psychographics, for instance, reveals that people between the ages of sixty-five and seventy are much less responsive than other age groups to direct-mail approaches. It also shows that teens are more likely to buy a product advertised as environmentally safe than one that makes no such claim.

Focus groups

An indispensable tool used by marketing researchers of all types is the focus group—generally consisting of a dozen or so members (either paid participants or volunteers). Focus group members usually are men and women representing a variety of ages, races, and ethnic and socioeconomic groups. Analysts use focus groups to determine people's opinions about and reactions to products and services before they are marketed widely. Similarly, commercials and political campaign speeches may be tried out on focus groups before receiving regional or nationwide exposure.

Sometimes, researchers use high-tech apparatus to track the physical reactions of focus group members to products, commercials, or pilot television shows. Among other things, researchers check for changes in perspiration, salivation, eye movements, brain waves, and voice patterns. Dilated pupils, for example, are said to indicate that the subject has great interest in some feature of a presentation.

Researchers are also experimenting with "smart devices"—optical scanning equipment that, when hooked onto a home television set, can identify any family mem-

bers who were watching the rigged TV when a certain advertisement was broadcast. Some focus groups already supply their members with handheld bar-code scanners that keep track of purchases made in stores. This information enables researchers to evaluate the effectiveness of certain TV commercials on consumer selections. The conclusions offered upon completion of such analyses are generally tentative, but many marketers find hints and clues more useful than no information at all.

How effective is advertising?

Do all the complex effort and expense that go into advertising make a difference? Some studies, for example, indicate that viewers soon forget 75 percent of the ads they see. Moreover, many observers think it is extremely difficult to prove that any specific ad or commercial deserves full credit for directly influencing anyone to buy a certain product. Max Sutherland, in his book *Advertising and the Mind of the Consumer: What Works, What Doesn't*

By studying focus groups, advertisers can determine the choices consumers are likely to make in the marketplace. If a product or commercial is not popular with a focus group, it is unlikely that the product will make it to the shelves or the commercial will make it on the air.

and Why, argues, "I don't think anyone believes that any ad will make them run out and buy the advertised product. Nothing has that kind of persuasive or coercive power."

What advertising really provides, continues Sutherland, are the "minor effects [that] tip the balance" in consumers' minds when they choose one brand over another. One advertising expert estimates that in a "normal marketing situation" up to fifty different factors can influence the sale of a product. For example, a person may decide to buy a new car not as a result of a commercial-stimulated desire to make a purchase but because his present vehicle is old and beyond repair. His monthly income, not an ad, may dictate the choice of a compact, rather than a luxury car. In fact, recommendations from trusted friends, the availability of service and parts, and the different reputations of local dealers may all influence the decision-making process. Yet in the end, when it is time to make a choice among similar models, it may be an effective ad that motivates the selection. An auto buyer might choose Ford over Toyota because the Ford ad—with its display of dedicated American assembly line workers—inspired in him a sense of patriotism.

Success stories

When a particular ad succeeds in a dramatic way, advertisers take notice. One popular success story in the advertising industry is that of Apple, the computer giant. Apple paid $2 million to televise a single 60-second spot during the 1984 Super Bowl game. Ten days after the event, the company had sold $100 million worth of computers. Experts credit the ad for generating the rush of sales.

For an earlier example of spectacular success of an advertisement, consider the following analysis by Lee Iacocca: The retired automotive industry executive believes that a thirty-six-page ad placed in one issue of the U.S. edition of *Reader's Digest* was responsible for generating the sales of tens of thousands of Ford Mustangs, back in the mid-1960s.

While businesspeople disagree over advertising's effectiveness, critics of the advertising industry think it works all too well.

Advertising's unexpected consequences

Some who monitor the ad industry say that advertising does more than influence buying decisions. These observers believe that with its many techniques and its relentless and widespread presence in daily life, advertising often succeeds in persuading people to be dissatisfied with what they have and then creating a hunger for things they don't really need. "The function of advertising," complains author Alice Embree, "has changed from the simple display of products and presentation of information to the

American society is saturated with commercial messages. Some critics believe these ever-present images have turned the United States into a nation of consumers who constantly hunger for products they do not need.

creation of needs. The bizarre consequence is the created 'need' for electric toothbrushes, wigs, false eyelashes, [and] an infinite variety of special cleansers."

Some thinkers even suggest that advertising encourages a new and undesirable way to live. Historian Christopher Lasch, in his book *The Culture of Narcissism*, argued:

> Advertising serves not so much to advertise products as to promote consumption as a way of life. It "educates" the masses into an unappeasable appetite not only for goods but for new experiences and personal fulfillment. It upholds consumption as the answer to the age-old discontents of loneliness, sickness, weariness, lack of sexual satisfaction; at the same time it creates new forms of discontent peculiar to the modern age.

Part of the problem, as critics see it, is that advertising has become inextricably woven into the country's social fabric. As Deborah Baldwin of *Common Cause* magazine puts it:

> Round-the-clock commercialism has crept up on us . . . [and has evolved] . . . into a sophisticated art form that pops up everywhere we are—from the brand-name labels that turn consumers into walking billboards to the corporate-sponsored informational posters that hang in classrooms.

An endless downpour of advertising messages saturates American society. One study reveals that the average American experiences as many as sixteen hundred commercial messages each day. Altogether, perhaps some 4.2 billion advertising messages are received by the American people every twenty-four hours. They appear on television, radio, box tops, billboards, buildings, sweatshirts, the Internet, telephone and fax lines, and even in public restrooms. Many trucks, subways, trains, and school buses carry ads. In 1995 ads for Mr. Chef's Famous Donuts appeared on squad cars in Oxnard, California, to raise money for the local police department.

Mass culture

"When we die we will have spent an estimated one and a half years just watching t.v. commercials," writes Max Sutherland. "No matter which way you look at it, advertising today takes up a significant chunk of our lives. For that reason, if for no other, advertising is an important phenomenon in our society."

Critics of mass culture insist that constant exposure to advertising, with its emphasis on buying and consuming, has led to a materialistic society whose members can all too easily lose their moral and spiritual bearings and begin to measure everything in life in terms of selling, buying, and consuming. "What are the implications of all this persuasion [advertising] in terms of our existing morality?" asked Vance Packard. "What does it mean for the national morality to have so many powerfully influential people [advertisers] taking a manipulative attitude toward our society?"

Media analysts also point out that virtually every major source of information—news, entertainment, politics, and even some areas of public education—is financially backed by advertisers, who serve as "sponsors." Even during the Persian Gulf War, many companies vied to have their products visibly associated with American troops.

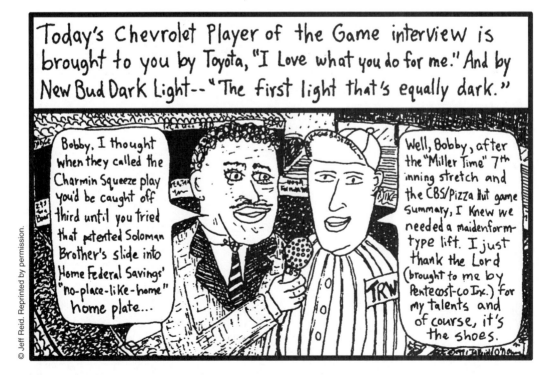

Leslie Savan, a long-time critic of advertising's more negative impact on society, complains in her book *The Sponsored Life: Ads, TV, and American Culture*:

> In short, we're living the sponsored life. From Huggies to Maalox, the necessities and little luxuries of an American's pass through this world are provided and promoted by one advertiser or another. The real masterwork of advertising is the way it uses the techniques of art to seduce the human soul. Virtually all of modern experience now has a sponsor, or at least a sponsored accessory, and there is no human emotion or concern—love, lust, war, childhood innocence, social rebellion, spiritual enlightenment, even disgust with advertising—that cannot be reworked into a sales pitch.

Despite such criticism, most advertisers use advertising for one reason only—it works. As Howard Morgan, former president of Procter & Gamble, once argued: "We believe that advertising is the most effective and efficient way to sell to the consumer. If we should ever find better methods of selling our type of products to the consumer, we'll leave advertising and turn to these other methods."

That's not likely to happen soon, however. For better or worse, advertising shows every sign of long remaining one of America's favorite ways to sell. Yet through all of the sales pitches, advertising must still convey a message, and how consumers judge the claims of that message is an important aspect of advertising's success or failure.

3

Truth in Advertising

W HEN PATIENTS MEET with their doctors, they expect to be told the truth. Similarly, a court of law demands that witnesses swear to be truthful. Pilots and passengers stake their lives on the truthfulness of the mechanics who certify that a jet aircraft is ready for takeoff.

The need for truth abounds in everyday life. It's essential for making sound decisions and establishing bonds of trust. But when it comes to advertising—one of the most widespread everyday activities in America—people are often uncertain. Should advertisers be held to the same high standard of truth as those whose statements may have life-or-death consequences? Or, do advertising claims somehow deserve to be accepted on the basis of lighter scrutiny?

Can advertising be completely truthful?

Because of its very nature, advertising may be harder to characterize as "true" or "false" than other products of human activity. "All advertising is inherently misleading," an ad critic once asserted. But this statement doesn't mean that all advertisers are deliberately deceptive. In fact, the great majority of advertisers try hard to be fair and honest in their dealings with the public. After all, they want to stay in business; but if consumers unmistakably express the belief that certain ads are deceptive, at best the agency that created the ads perceived to be untruthful will be fired, and at worst the company whose products were thought to be misrepresented will fail.

Nonetheless, the act of selling often misleads consumers. Writers of advertising copy—the text portion of an ad—are not journalists or historians whose main purpose is to supply readers with facts. Instead, they represent businesspeople whose foremost goal is to earn a profit. This calls for ads capable of persuading consumers that a given product, service, or company is better than all rivals. And like any advocate, people who create ads try to accentuate the good characteristics of what they are selling. Sometimes this means that they brag and exaggerate. They may also omit the mention of facts about a product that might turn consumers away.

This 1950s advertisement claims that L&M cigarettes are "just what the doctor ordered." Ad copywriters try to highlight a product's good qualities, such as filters in the case of L&M cigarettes, while downplaying any negative aspects.

Few Americans are surprised or dismayed to find out that ads and commercials tend to favor one company or brand over another. It is assumed that most sales pitches are nothing more than organized cheers for a certain product or company. Few consumers, for example, take seriously a restaurant's claim to have "the best barbecue in the South." Nor do they expect animated cartoon characters to appear on the kitchen table when they open a box of cereal.

Consumers do, of course, object to being lied to or fed misleading statements, but it isn't always clear just where acceptable exaggeration ends and deception begins. For help in making such judgments with confidence, consumers have turned increasingly to the government.

What advertisers can do

Throughout much of the history of the United States, the unwritten rule that governed business transactions was the Latin phrase *Caveat emptor*—"Let the buyer beware." Custom decreed that it was up to a prospective purchaser to use an appropriate degree of skepticism when confronted by advertising claims of various sellers. Sellers assumed no responsibility for any defects in products that they sold. Consumers made their purchases without any warranties or guarantees made by the sellers.

As a result of the consumer protection movement, which began in the early part of this century, however, a host of federal laws now govern advertising. In addition, every state except Louisiana has implemented as part of its statutes the Uniform Commercial Code (UCC), a set of standards that identify the rights and responsibilities of those who are engaged in business. Added to these and other state laws are many local ordinances that regulate advertising.

Despite having considerable freedom to promote their products, advertisers must comply with the UCC. For example, producers must label their goods, listing the materials used in making the items. Moreover, these materials must match any advertising claims advanced about the contents of the products. Advertisers are forbidden to engage in selling tricks such as "bait and switch"—the practice of advertising a desirable product at a low price but pressuring customers lured into the shop by the ads to accept an inferior item, or one that is more expensive. Finally, advertisements that are blatantly untrue are forbidden. For instance, it is illegal under the UCC to make false claims about the quality or performance of a product.

Often, though, it is difficult to discern the difference between deception and puffery—overblown salesmanship. For example, an ad that says a certain car is the best on the road will be interpreted by most consumers as biased opinion; but a claim that a car gets fifty miles to the gallon when it really gets half that amount is deceptive. And it's this kind of deception—especially when it leads consumers to waste their money, hurt themselves, or, even worse, lose their lives—that sends government officials into action.

Deliberately deceitful

Among the most seriously deceptive ads are those that promise a lot and deliver nothing. This is a type of theft. Thus scam artists who advertise phony stock investment schemes, opportunities to make money working at nonexistent jobs, sweepstakes contests that nobody wins, or any number of other bogus offerings are lawbreakers.

In other cases, goods or services are indeed available to the consumer, but they are not what the ads promised. Products promoted by means of such deceptive ads include disposable diapers that don't deteriorate in ninety days as advertised, electronic devices that consistently malfunction, tools that break when used as directed, and antiwrinkle creams that fail to ward off signs of old age.

Of special concern to industry monitors are ads that deceive consumers in matters of health and safety. Such was the case in 1990 when Volvo, the Swedish car manufacturer, ran a television ad depicting one of its autos outperforming a rival in a crash safety test. But there was something the ad didn't disclose. As Anne G. Perkins noted in the *Harvard Business Review*, "The Volvo that survived that crash had a notable advantage over its wrecked competitor; it had been reinforced with steel." After consumer advocate and TV celebrity David Horowitz revealed the hoax, the agency responsible for the ad gave up its account with Volvo. Subsequently, the automaker tried to polish its tarnished image with yet another advertising campaign.

Confusing and insupportable claims

Outright phony claims in advertising are relatively easy to unmask. But in many cases, it is much harder to pinpoint the actual deceptive parts, especially when the copy is ambiguous or imprecise. Phrases such as "new and improved," so commonly used by advertisers, may mean little or nothing at all. Consumers are often left wondering: Newer than what? Improved over what?

Some claims may be only partially true, or insupportable, as in the case of a recent TV commercial that claimed a certain high-fiber cereal was a good preventive against "cancer." The commercial was denounced by some as being misleading. It may be true that a high-fiber cereal is somewhat effective in warding off cancer of the colon; but it is false to imply, as the ad in question did, that the client's brand could help prevent all cancers.

Government officials scrutinize such claims and often take legal action against producers of ads that mislead the public. For example, Procter & Gamble was cited by New York City officials for falsely advertising that its Citrus Hill orange juice, which is made from concentrate, was fresh.

Exploiting trends

Advertising copywriters often choose words aimed at exploiting trends and end up misleading the public. During the early 1990s, for instance, advertisers tried to cash in on a widespread concern for the environment. Soon the marketplace teemed with ecologically correct advertising campaigns. Some marketers even packaged their products in green wrappings and labels to make them appealing to consumers wanting to help the environment. Many ads boasted of products that were "biodegradable." Multinational corporations filled Sunday morning television broadcasts with commercials in which the companies appeared to be taking action to help the environment.

Though some of these commercial messages were accurate, many were either meaningless or misleading. According to Greenpeace writers Debra Lynn Dadd and André Carothers:

> The environmental advertising bandwagon offers companies an opportunity to spruce up their images at relatively low cost. Many of the recycled paper products now flooding the market are made by companies with otherwise reprehensible [deserving of serious criticism] environmental records. . . . These companies rely on governmental regulations for some of their claims, leading to situations like McDonald's declaration that their styrofoam burger trays are CFC-free, when in fact they contain CFC-22, a less potent member of the

same chemical family [of chlorofluorocarbons, suspected of playing a role in the depletion of the ozone layer]. . . . All this should raise doubts about industry's claims that they have seen the light, and that hiding behind the advertising pitch is a real concern for the environment that transcends the bottom line.

Also in recent years, Americans exhibited a fascination with "natural" foods and health. In response, many advertisers tout their merchandise as having healthful-sounding attributes. Store shelves now teem with food products said to be "low-fat" or "high-fiber"; "all natural ingredients" is another frequent claim. Yet the use of such words in advertising copy doesn't necessarily indicate deliberate attempts at deception. Sometimes there is honest confusion over what the terms mean. Writer Alexandra Greeley uses the example of Sara Lee's "light classic" cheesecake to show how a typical consumer's understanding may fail to match the copywriter's intent:

Naturally, with a name like ["light"], most dieters thought the cheesecake was a calorie- and fat-reduced product suitable for weight-reduction programs. That was a reasonable assumption, but consumers did not realize that manufacturers may also use the word light to refer to the color, taste, or content of other high-calorie ingredients. In the case of the cheesecake, Sara Lee used light to describe texture. In fact, this product contains more calories than Sara Lee's original cheesecake.

To end this confusion, in 1992 the federal Departments of Agriculture and Health and Human Services produced four thousand pages of regulations spelling out new rules and definitions that advertisers must apply when they mention product content on packaging labels. Among other things, advertisers now need to have scientific evidence to prove their claims.

Commercials in sheep's clothing?

Sometimes untruth in advertising is hard to detect because the promotional copy is camouflaged by another form of communication. When this happens, consumers have trouble deciding where the news or entertainment ends and

During his broadcasts, radio personality Paul Harvey often blurred the distinction between his news commentary and commercial messages. Even though advertisers continue to use this strategy, critics argue that it makes it difficult for consumers to separate fact from fiction.

the sales pitch begins. Smudging the line between entertainment and commercials is nothing new. During the early days of television, talk show hosts often read both the news and the commercials. Sometimes the two tasks overlapped. Paul Harvey, a well-known radio personality, habitually worked commercials into his news commentary without changing tempo to indicate the switch.

Today the trend continues ever stronger. In fact, there is "an increasingly blurred line between programming and ads on network television," writes ad critic Leslie Savan. "Of course, the ad-driven medium has never been a pristine art form, its practitioners not generally averse to bending over backward to please sponsors. But lately, advertising's osmotic bleed [subtle intrusion] into entertainment has turned into an arterial gush [large-scale invasion]."

"Product placement"

That line of separation has disappeared altogether in many cases. For many TV programs, advertising has become part of the TV show itself—whether it is a drama, sitcom, or musical variety. For a price, plugs for products, attacks on a sponsor's competitor, and a host of other messages are commonly written into TV scripts. Publicizing merchandise—called "product placement"—also occurs in motion pictures, as many advertisers negotiate with film producers to have their products mentioned or seen as backdrops in movies. Observes Deborah Baldwin: "According to one tally, the creative minds behind *Die Hard 2* found room for 19 paid ads. When one company, Black & Decker, discovered 'its' scene on the cutting room floor, it sued for $150,000."

Though such practices are not necessarily meant to deceive consumers, they do smudge the border between advertising and entertainment. Audiences are generally unaware that included in the price of a movie theater ticket are unexpected advertisements. Traditionally commercials in movie theaters are shown before or after a film—not during it. Even this practice evokes the ire of some consumers who believe that their ticket purchase entitles them to enjoy an entertainment without being subjected to sales pitches at all.

In addition, many unsophisticated viewers, especially young children, may falsely assume that celebrities use certain products portrayed in films. This may entice children to purchase items that they believe are being endorsed by their cinematic role models, even though that celebrity probably has no control over which products are "placed" in the film.

And even literate adults inevitably may have their impressions of products subtly shaped and reinforced by product placements—something they presumably did not

One of the California Raisins sings during a commercial in a movie theater. Although commercials like this are generally shown before or after a movie, advertisers can also pay to have their products placed inside the film.

seek for themselves when they purchased tickets for an entertainment.

Meanwhile, another trend is fast developing on television that signals the complete collapse of a line of separation between programming and advertising—the infomercial.

Infomercials: hybrid ads

Joe Saltzman, associate mass media editor of *USA Today*, provides this description of infomercials:

> Usually 30 minutes long, infomercials are out to sell viewers products that you probably never heard about, often featuring a personality or celebrity you *have* heard about. These are the only TV programs in history that are one long commercial that breaks for short commercials for the very same product.

At first glance, an infomercial appears to be regular TV fare—a chatty talk show, or a bodybuilding or cooking program. But its real purpose soon becomes clear: Infomercials try to hook the attention of viewers and persuade them to call an 800 number to purchase cosmetics, bodybuilding equipment, food slicers, or other mail-order products.

Normally found on early weekend morning hours on cable TV stations, infomercials offer tempting advantages to advertisers. For one thing, compared to thirty-second commercial spots, there is plenty of time to get a point across. Infomercials are also more cost-effective than shorter ads. Another advantage of the infomercial, writes Lionel Fisher in the *Oregonian*, is that "it literally can count its successes. Each ad's effectiveness is instantly verified by the number of 800 calls it generates. Capable of collecting valuable direct-mail lists at relatively low cost, infomercials double as an effective data-gathering tool."

Increasingly, major marketers ranging from political organizations to companies such as Volvo, AT&T, General Motors, and Apple Computer are turning to infomercials to advertise. In 1995 Cox Cable Communications and Jones International Networks joined forces to create a twenty-four-hour infomercial channel.

But as infomercials proliferate, they are fast attracting the attention of industry watchdogs. Critics say that infomercials are nothing but full-blown commercials masquerading as regular programs that can dupe the unwary. In fact, the government has already taken legal action against some infomercial producers. In 1993 the Federal Trade Commission (FTC) fined Regal Communications $3.5 million for fraudulent TV claims that its products improved cellulite conditions and cured baldness. During the same year, the FTC fined National Media $275,000 for using an infomercial to advance the false claim that one of its products cured breast cancer.

Government regulation

Across the United States, hundreds of government watchdogs examine the words and images of advertisements. In addition to regulatory departments in every state government, there are many federal agencies that monitor the advertising industry. Primary responsibility for dealing with deceptive ads falls to the FTC. Although the government does not screen commercial messages before they appear to the public, once an ad surfaces that FTC officials determine is deceptive, false, or misleading, the commission can require the company to sign a consent order—a voluntary agreement to stop the offending advertisement. If the company refuses, the FTC can then issue a cease-and-desist order that compels the advertiser to withdraw the material or face substantial fines.

Sometimes, the FTC requires an advertiser to show advertising substantiation, or proof that the claims made in the ads are true. When a company is unable to do this, the FTC can demand an affirmative disclosure. This statement, which describes the product's limitations, must be clearly displayed during the advertisement.

In addition, the FTC has the authority to order a company to run "corrective advertising" to inform the public that earlier ads were false. This power was exercised in 1972 when the FTC investigated advertising claims by the Warner-Lambert Company that its Listerine mouthwash helped prevent colds and sore throats. When the FTC determined that this claim was both misleading and false, Warner-Lambert was forced to run a corrective ad that said: "Listerine will not help prevent colds or sore throats or lessen their severity."

As strict as these rules appear, the FTC is hardly overzealous. Out of the estimated million ads and commercials the FTC is asked to review each year, it puts a stop to only about five hundred. This figure represents only about 0.05 percent of the ads scrutinized by the commission. Most cases are settled before they reach a court.

Advertisers also face scrutiny from other federal regulatory authorities. Inspectors for the Food and Drug Administration (FDA), for instance, watch the advertising of pharmaceuticals and the labeling used by food product companies. Meanwhile, the Federal Communications Commission (FCC) supervises advertising on television, radio, and wire communications media, focusing particularly on commercials aimed at children. The Securities and Exchange Commission (SEC) checks for deceptive advertising of stocks and bonds, while the U.S. Postal Service prosecutes those who use the mail to distribute deceptive advertising. The Consumer Product Safety Commission and the U.S. Office of Consumer Affairs are among the other agencies that regulate some aspects of advertising.

Consumer advocates

Government officials aren't the only ones who keep an eye on the advertising industry. Many private consumer organizations, such as the Consumers Union in the United States, monitor advertising and publish their findings. Organizations such as the Friends of the Earth also keep tabs on marketing claims of ads that touch on environmental issues.

Although this long line of ad watchers displeases some in the industry who object to what they see as a meddlesome presence, many advertisers welcome regulation as a way of promoting order and fairness in what might otherwise be a chaotic marketplace.

Advertising, like most major industries, also tries to police its own ranks. For example, the American Association of Advertising Agencies asks its members to heed a code of ethics in advertising. The National Advertising Review Board reviews questionable ads and accepts complaints from consumers concerning advertising. Many publishers and broadcasters also maintain written guidelines that clarify what constitutes appropriate advertising. In addition, most Better Business Bureau offices across the United States investigate complaints of deceptive advertising and notify government officials if corrective action is deemed necessary but not taken.

Part of modern life?

All this monitoring of advertising brings under scrutiny some important American values. Americans place a high premium on freedom. And they also expect fairness and honesty in their dealings with others. But in a free society these values often collide—especially in the marketplace,

A department store clerk helps a customer decide between different housewares. Despite regulations about truth in advertising, consumers cannot rely on advertising alone to supply important information about products.

where advertisers enjoy great freedom in what they can say in their ads.

Increasingly, advocacy organizations are insisting that consumers have rights and are demanding recognition of, for example, the right to receive a product that functions as advertised. Advocacy groups also assert that consumers are entitled to know the truth about products being sold, since only a well-informed person can make good purchasing decisions.

The tension generated between advertisers and consumers is typical of many free-market countries. Invariably, the question arises: How far should government go in regulating advertising? Too much government can interfere with the operation of free markets. On the other hand, too little invites fraud and abuse of consumers' trust. Alan Thein Durning, a senior researcher at the World Watch Institute, says that a major task for all democracies is "to decide how much advertising to tolerate, and while respecting the rights of individuals to speak their minds, to place appropriate limits on marketing."

Striking that delicate balance is increasingly important as the line between deception and truth in advertising becomes harder to distinguish.

4

Advertising and the Youth Market

WITH THEIR ABILITY to target any segment of society, many advertisers have set their sights on one of the world's most lucrative and controversial markets—America's youth. Why make an all-out effort to target the young? For one thing, children watch a lot of television. One estimate holds that by the time the average American child starts first grade he or she has spent the equivalent of three years watching TV, advertising's most powerful medium. As a result of this exposure, children begin at an early age to plead for the things they see on television, exerting, in turn, a lot of sway over parents and grandparents. In fact, "children ages 4–10 influence more than $131 billion of their parents' spending power each year," according to a brochure from Lifetime Learning System, a company that specializes in advertising to the youth market.

America's children aren't limited to pestering adults to buy them things; they have a lot of their own money to spend. In 1995 children between the ages of four and twelve spent $17 billion on consumer products.

Children, however, make up only part of the youth market. Teens also command attention from advertisers, but for different reasons. Particularly important to many advertisers is the existence of an age group characterized in many cases by the need to create self-identity and to impress peers. Thus teens are more likely to be influenced by images portrayed by advertisers in magazines aimed solely at them, on TV, at rock concerts, and at sporting events.

Though manufacturers of toys and fad items concentrate on selling their products to consumers while they are young, others target the youth market as a means of cultivating customer loyalty that will last well into adulthood. Studies show, for example, that children as young as four begin to choose among brands of toothpaste, cereal, and other products. Thus, many advertisers view their wooing of America's youth as a long-term and potentially lucrative investment.

Marketing to the young

And because advertisers stand to earn a lot from the youth market, they eagerly pursue it. Every day in the United States, advertisers produce about thirty thousand commercial messages aimed at young people. Using sophisticated marketing and research practices—focus groups, surveys, demographic and psychographic studies, and so on—advertisers try to find out what products youthful consumers will respond to. They then deliver their commercial messages in several ways. Often, they advertise in children's magazines such as *Sports Illustrated for Kids*, *Kid City*, and *Boys' Life* to sell drinks, cereal, toys, baseball cards, video games, and bubble gum. Other publications, such as *Seventeen* and *Sassy*, target teens with ads for products such as clothes, CDs, and personal care items.

Advertisers are also able to deliver their commercial messages by sponsoring sporting exhibitions, rodeos, concerts, and other events that attract crowds of young people. Commercials directed at the youth market can be found on billboards, on rental videos, and at motion picture theaters. Even direct mail is used to market children's products, including magazines, reference books, dolls, and clothes.

Like other advertisers, those who target the country's youth use demographic data to help them locate potential customers. But more and more marketers are realizing that they don't need to look too hard to find captive audiences.

As never before, advertisers are heading to school—where the youth market is conveniently concentrated.

Taking ads to school

With an estimated $81 billion student market waiting to be tapped, advertisers have a big incentive to break into America's schools. And many financially strapped school districts openly welcome associations with companies willing to pay or barter for the privilege of making campus sales pitches. As a result, millions of students encounter a variety of youth-related ads on huge colorful posters located in school cafeterias, in hallways, at entrances, and on athletic field scoreboards. Some campus television productions now broadcast commercials for tuxedos and prom dresses along with the morning announcements.

In addition, more than twelve thousand companies try to entice teachers with inexpensive or free "educational" materials such as booklets, brochures, films, and videos.

Though some of the resources are informative and useful, most are thinly disguised ads promoting a one-sided view that favors the sponsoring company or organization. For example, a "science" lesson from a Campbell's Soup text asks students to test whether another Campbell's product, its spaghetti sauce, is thicker than Ragu's.

Although some teachers welcome the resources provided free or at low cost by commercial enterprises, and believe they can use them carefully, *Consumer Reports*, the magazine of Consumers Union, the advocacy organization, thinks that the use of such materials in schools creates harm by making it "harder for students to discriminate between news and advertising, between the infomercial and the independent report, or between fact and fancy."

Channel One

One company has been penetrating the student market by beaming commercials directly into North America's secondary classrooms via Channel One—a ten-minute TV news program designed especially for teens. The program is free. In addition, Channel One offers an array of premiums—such as access to satellite transmission, VCRs, and TVs—to schools that subscribe to the broadcast. But in return, school officials must promise that 90 percent of the student body will watch the daily broadcasts and two minutes of advertising.

By the end of 1996, the Channel One program was viewed in 350,000 middle school and high school classrooms across the United States—a figure that represents as much as 40 percent of the nation's students in this age group. Many critics are alarmed by this trend. They argue that once Channel One has entered a school, profit-minded businesspeople, not educators, decide what topics will be presented, and when. The use of students as a captive audience at a tax-supported institution is another source of critics' disapproval.

Supporters of Channel One, however, suggest that exposure to two minutes of advertising a day is a small sacrifice in exchange for a chance to use high-tech equipment. They also point out that advertising in schools is nothing new: Library shelves are filled with magazines and newspapers that carry ads.

Aside from the controversy it arouses, the use of television at school to tap the student market marks a new trend in advertising. Many see the growing presence on campus of TV advertising as a logical extension of the advertising industry's most effective means of capturing the attention of America's youth.

TV advertising

Since almost all television broadcasting in the United States is done for commercial purposes, advertisers dominate the airwaves and have an unprecedented level of access to most of the nation's young. After all, children and teens do not read the same magazines or attend the same sports events and entertainments, but virtually all of them watch television. One study reveals that children between the ages of six and eighteen spend more time watching TV than engaging in any other activity. As a result, an average young TV viewer could possibly see as many as twenty thousand thirty-second commercials in one year. It is not surprising, then, that television advertisers spend well over $800 million a year just on TV ads aimed at America's youth. Most of these ads appear on Saturday mornings and after school hours, when children are most likely to be watching TV.

What makes TV so convenient for advertisers—and maddening to their critics—is that children provide a ready-made audience. Watching Saturday morning television shows is common practice for millions of children.

Because young people make up a large portion of television viewers, advertisers spend over $800 million a year trying to inform and influence them about consumer choices.

Advertising sponsors present a multitude of kid-centered programs to young viewers; but crammed between short segments of these news, education, and entertainment features are glitzy, fast-paced commercials for toys, clothes, candy, and breakfast cereals. And because advertisers know from research that animation is one of the most effective ways of keeping young minds focused on a given message, cartoons galore appear on the nation's screens imploring children to eat (or at least buy) candy, cookies, and bubble gum.

Advertisers do make possible many shows that are both entertaining and informative, but they also create and sell programs that are little more than extended ads. Typically, long on action and short on plot, these shows feature characters available as dolls or action figures at any toy store. Barbie, GI Joe, He-Man, Super-Cats, Strawberry Shortcake, Teenage Mutant Ninja Turtles, and Power Rangers are just some of the products that have doubled as television characters and commercial merchandise in recent years. Many critics of children's television believe that by using fantasy characters in this way, advertisers blur the line between entertainment and advertising. And in the process, children are exposed to even more advertising.

Public concern, government action

In recent years, public concern has prompted the federal government to take action. Thus, today, the FCC requires broadcasters to maintain a strict wall of separation between advertising and entertainment offerings. Nonetheless, some broadcasters still challenge the rule. In 1992, for example, the Fox Network announced plans to feature the cartoon character Chester Cheetah in an animated series. This announcement rankled Action for Children's Television (ACT), a private organization that, among other things, fights to protect children from exploitative TV advertising. ACT pointed out that Fox was violating the FCC rule because Chester Cheetah was originally a well-known advertising figure used to promote Frito-Lay's Chee-tos snack. As a result of the complaint, Fox canceled its plans.

Is marketing to children ethical?

The concerns of ACT and similarly minded groups underscore an important recurring question in modern advertising: Is it fair and ethical to target children with ads? Most advertisers see nothing wrong in marketing aggressively to the young. Honest businesspeople with products for children and teens do not think they should be prevented from letting the public know what they have for sale. In addition, it is often suggested that advertising provides useful consumer information for children and parents alike.

But many who monitor the ad industry disagree with these assessments. For one thing, they don't like the idea of children being targeted by business groups that far surpass them in sophistication and knowledge of sales techniques. Critics generally believe that the country's youth—especially the very young—are much more susceptible than adults to the power of advertising. Unlike adults, young children often fail to see the difference between programming and commercials. In fact, TV advertising may hinder them in their earliest attempts to make sense of the real world. Nancy S. Maldonado, assistant professor at Lehman College of the City University of New York, argues that "commercials present an unrealistic view of the world that contributes to a . . . child's inability to distinguish fantasy from reality."

And because TV commercials aimed at children use a variety of entertainment techniques—humor, adventure, catchy music, cartoons, appealing toys, flashy graphics—young viewers often watch the commercials and regular programming with equal interest. In fact, "children like commercials, and corporations know how to take advantage of this sad fact of TV life," says Peggy Charren, founder of ACT. This means that, as a rule, children don't press the mute button or change channels when commercials appear. Instead, they watch attentively, giving advertisers enough time to make their sales pitches.

A 1989 study of the impact of commercials on children conducted by Towson State University professor Ellen

Notar reveals that commercials aimed at children are often louder than normal programming, are repeated over and over, and take up as much as 25 percent of every hour of TV viewing. The net effect of these efforts is both to snag the attention of children and to reinforce the commercial messages.

Such heavy exposure, suggest critics of advertising practices, encourages America's youth not only to want

A mother and daughter shop for dolls during a visit to the toy store. Most critics of advertising believe that children are highly vulnerable to commercial messages and have trouble distinguishing between entertainment and ads.

products they see on TV, but also to develop a materialistic view of life at an impressionable age. The *Wall Street Journal* quotes a children's marketing expert who says "Even two-year-olds are concerned about their brand of clothes, and by the age of six are full-out consumers."

Children, television, and parental supervision

Given the rise of dual-income and single-parent households, many children today spend hours alone in front of a TV set. Without parental guidance and supervision, however, they may be highly vulnerable to persuasive TV advertising techniques. In the early 1980s advertisers learned to profit from this vulnerability by making commercials that promoted 900-number telephone services. Most children old enough to dial their own phone calls are aware that calls to 800 numbers are free. Many, however, do not understand that calls to a 900 number are billed by the minute. Several sets of California parents learned of this knowledge gap the hard way when a salesman dressed as Santa began appearing in local television spots. Children were told that they could dial a 900 number to get a daily Christmas story, and a few young callers made toll calls costing hundreds of dollars without their parents' knowledge.

Attorney Robert Gnaizda of the citizens' group Public Advocates, Inc., reports that 900-number companies that target children gleaned as much as $200 million from California children in 1990 alone. Moreover, he estimated in 1990 that as much as $2 billion is taken in annually nationwide by advertisers who target kids with 900-number appeals. These advertisers, he says, "know that most of the money will be made from repeated unauthorized calls largely from low income persons, from latch-key children, from language deficient children and from new immigrants who do not understand 900 numbers."

California is not alone, however. In recent years, other 900-number companies across the country have urged children to call up the Easter Bunny and Woody Woodpecker.

Children's vulnerability to advertising may be also bad for their health. Experts have concluded that a distressing number of TV commercials aimed at kids try to persuade them to buy and eat food that is not good for them. A 1995 report from the University of Minnesota reveals that during fifty hours of Saturday morning children's programs broadcast on ABC, CBS, Fox, and Nickelodeon, some one thousand commercials were aired—but not one encouraged young viewers to eat vegetables and fruits. Instead, researchers found that much of what was being advertised was processed food containing high levels of saturated fat and refined sugar.

While watching television, children are faced with a barrage of commercials. In addition to advertisements for games and toys, children also encounter numerous commercials for candy and junk food, which many critics fear endanger children's health.

Tufts University's *Diet & Nutrition Letter* from the same year agreed that "when millions of American children tune into the Saturday morning television spree each week . . . [they watch] . . . a steady stream of commercial pitches for sugar-coated cereals, fatty fast food, candy, soda pop, and other items of limited nutritional value."

The American Academy of Pediatrics Committee on Communications is concerned by statistics indicating that children watch so many ads for so-called junk food: "Because young children cannot understand the relationship between food choices and chronic nutritional disease, advertising food products to children promotes profit rather than health." Organizations such as the physicians' group just quoted believe these commercials should be eliminated, but advertisers insist that it is their right to promote legal products. It is the consumer's responsibility, advertisers state, to choose which products or services they will purchase.

How susceptible are children to advertising?

Much of the concern over children's advertising centers on a fear that youngsters are easily manipulated by ads. But some advertisers respond that kids may be less susceptible than some critics think. According to at least one study, children quickly learn that toys are seldom as exciting as portrayed in ads. This discovery teaches them to be more discriminating when faced with future ads. Glen Smith, at one time a managing director of the marketing group Children's Research Unit, says: "We find that children are aware of the purposes of advertising at a very early age, and that they apply their own quite stringent criteria when evaluating advertisements."

Many advertisers add that although they sell products to the youth market, they are not exploiting children. They remind parents who worry about overexposure of their children to TV advertising that they can always turn the set off. In addition, advertisers suggest that parents teach children to cultivate resistance to advertising pitches.

Some dismiss the claim that children aren't affected by commercial messages. Why, they ask, do companies bother to advertise if commercials make no impact on children? They also argue that children are indeed vulnerable because they are young, inexperienced, and immature. This point is amplified by Newton N. Minow and

Craig L. LaMay, in their book *Abandoned in the Waste-land: Children, Television and the First Amendment:*

> [W]hile adults can take full responsibility for themselves, children typically cannot. They do not have the skills, resources or knowledge to make the normal market mechanism related to consumer choice meaningful, which means that others—parents, educators, physicians, judges, librarians, and so on—must play a role in making meaningful choices for them.

For these reasons, many adults believe that easily impressed children need special protection from advertisers, just as they would from any other adults who try to unduly influence them. In fact, a survey in a 1991 issue of *Advertising Age* magazine showed that 62 percent of respondents favored a total ban on the broadcasting of advertising aimed at children.

The argument that older youth need special protection is harder to make. Teens, after all, are hardly as susceptible as toddlers. On the threshold of adulthood, they often pride themselves on being able to make wise consumer choices. Nonetheless, because of their lack of experience, many teens are more vulnerable to advertising than they realize. Some still lack the maturity to distinguish between industry-driven images and their own needs. The truth of this assertion has been borne out in recent years by the rash of extreme cases involving teens so desperate to own sports shoes advertised as highly prestigious that they have beaten up and even killed other teens to get a pair.

Thus, advertisers know that many teens are easily influenced by advertising, albeit in ways quite different from those typical of their younger counterparts.

Targeting teens

Since most teens are beginning to earn their own money, they are able to make many of their own purchases. In 1992 total income for U.S. youth ages fourteen to seventeen was $34.7 billion—a sum that makes this set of consumers enormously attractive to marketers.

    Though many teens tend to break away from the author-
ity of adults and strive for independence, they must con-
tend with attempts to influence them from another
source—namely, their peers. Because teens spend much of
their time with people their own age, peer pressure to con-
form is strong. As a result, many teens worry about not being able to keep pace with others. To fit in with their
contemporaries, they may decide to wear the latest fashion, cut their hair a certain way, or own a popular type of
CD player or skateboard.

Though many teens do imitate others, they also try to figure out who they are as individuals. At times, this personal quest leads them to experiment with different lifestyles and fashions. And as always, advertisers are ready to provide a variety of images to choose from. Teens can be found portrayed in magazines or on television as Olympic-bound athletes, gangster rappers, risk-taking daredevils, members of Seattle-based grunge bands, country western music fans, supermodels, or clean-cut preppies. All these images, different from one another as they are, try to glorify a lifestyle suggested by the ads and persuade teens to buy the merchandise that is presented as being a part of that world.

Advertising and adolescence

The teenage years are also a period of dramatic physical and emotional transformation as young people mature into adulthood. All this tension causes uncertainty and doubts about personal appearance and helps make teens vulnerable to solutions offered by the mass media. Advertisers try to address adolescent needs, fears, and doubts by filling the pages of teen magazines with colorful ads for makeup, complexion aids, special diets, jeans, and sports shoes. These products also sponsor TV shows that attract teen viewers. Some advertisers, in fact, have become the financial backbone of entire TV networks such as MTV and VH-1 whose singular purpose is to target young adults.

Many teens wonder whether their bodies will ever measure up to the standards of feminine beauty or male attractiveness portrayed and promoted by the mass media. Since, however, one longtime advertising strategy has been to create in consumers feelings of dissatisfaction about themselves, success is often hard to achieve. At times, teens become so distressed that they will try almost anything to change their appearance.

Understanding these frustrations all too well, some advertisers use teen magazines to promote items that promise to alleviate adolescent woes. Many of the products are worthless or harmful. Some of the most questionable ads are those that try to convince underdeveloped teenage girls that special devices, exercise programs, even creams will enlarge their breasts. None of these measures works, say FDA officials. According to an agency bulletin, "The only proven method of increasing breast size is breast augmentation surgery, which carries some risk and is hardly recommended for teenagers."

The FDA also frowns on many other ads that urge teens to send away for diet products such as pills and body wraps to lose weight. The agency also carefully scrutinizes ads for tanning pills and hair-removal creams. Many of these items have been found to have dangerous side effects, and their manufacturers were ordered to pull them from the market.

During the teenage years, young people are often concerned about their appearance and are vulnerable to advertising that promises to transform their image.

Not all "teen" products, of course, are dangerous, but many nonetheless fall far short of their implied promises of glory, popularity, attractive dates, and good times.

Tempting teens to smoke and drink

Some of the harshest criticism of advertisers who target the young is leveled at sellers of tobacco and alcoholic beverages. Critics charge that some marketers try to entice young people to drink and smoke well before the legal age by making these activities appear to be glamorous and fun. Again is heard the argument that advertisers zero in on young people because they are susceptible. Antismoking activists are especially incensed by the Philip Morris Company's use of Joe Camel, a "cool-looking" cartoon character who has acquired many fans among children and

In the Bronx, a billboard advertising Camel cigarettes in Spanish shows the company's mascot, Joe Camel, who it says is "a smooth character." Many people worry that ads like this one target young people and encourage them to smoke by using cartoon characters and by glamorizing smoking.

teens. Though the tobacco company claims that Joe Camel is meant for adults, the federal Centers for Disease Control and Prevention reports that between 1988, when the Joe Camel campaign began, and 1995, teenage preference for Camels increased 300 percent. Such a finding dovetails with research gleaned by John P. Pierce of the University of California, San Diego. A coauthor of a study on the causes of smoking, Dr. Pierce argues that "Tobacco marketing is much stronger than peer pressure in getting a youngster to take the first step toward smoking. It is what starts adolescents down the slippery slope to addiction."

Spokespersons for the tobacco industry often respond to such accusations by referring to a 1991 Gallup poll indicating that children's decisions to smoke were based more on peer pressure and access to tobacco products than on advertising. But this rejoinder hardly proves that advertising plays no role in the effort to recruit new smokers.

Though ads for tobacco products are illegal on television, and hard liquor companies generally observe a voluntary self-imposed ban on TV commercials, alcohol and tobacco companies have at their disposal plenty of other advertising outlets, including magazines and newspapers, billboards and posters. Beer companies, for instance, sponsor staged events directed at teenagers and young adults such as rock concerts, spring break parties at Daytona Beach, sporting events, and dance contests. These

In addition to advertising on television, in magazines, and on billboards, alcohol companies like Colt 45 (pictured) can promote their products by sponsoring sporting exhibitions, concerts, and other events.

commercial sponsors are quick to claim that by underwriting the costs of such events, they are helping to stage events for the public—events that might not take place without their financial support. But they may be contributing to the problem of teen drinking as well. Judy Monroe in the magazine *Current Health 2* points out that "although alcohol ads feature adults and are purportedly geared to adult viewers, teens see them, too. By age 18, the average American teen will have seen 100,000 TV beer commercials. Yet in all 50 states and the District of Columbia, the legal drinking age is 21."

Monroe also observes that according to many experts these ads "encourage underage drinking, establish loyalty to a brand early, so that a teen will continue to drink a particular brand for life, [and] have contributed to the current rise in teen alcoholism."

Despite these assertions, however, researchers find it hard to prove conclusively that a direct link exists between advertising and consumption or use of dangerous products by young people. Still, many wonder why advertising aimed at influencing adults wouldn't also be effective with minors.

An ongoing effort

The same arguments against tobacco and alcoholic beverage ads allegedly targeting youth often are raised concerning advertising in the youth market in general. What concerns many parents, educators, and child advocates is the tremendous amount of effort some advertisers put into selling to young Americans. Many social critics accuse the business community of viewing the nation's children as just another market segment to be researched, targeted, and sold to by corporate advertisers. But with billions of dollars in disposable income in the hands of the young, advertisers cannot afford to neglect this influential segment of the American economy.

5

Advertising and Politics

"WITH PUBLIC OPINION on its side, nothing can fail," Abraham Lincoln declared. These presidential words still ring true. Today anyone who hopes to be successful in politics must first master the sophisticated techniques of shaping public opinion. And the most effective way to reach millions of busy voters spread across America is through advertising. In fact, advertising may be indispensable to those wishing to achieve political power in the modern world. Winston Fletcher, a British advertiser, made this comment about elections in America: "Without advertising, Dewey lost; with advertising, Eisenhower won. Ergo [therefore], advertising wins elections."

Advertising's role in politics

As in the world of business, the most powerful advertising medium available to politicians is television. Ever since the TV set became a household fixture in the United States of the 1950s, political candidates have been marketed much like any other commodity. Former national Republican Party chairman Leonard Hall once observed, "You sell your candidates and your programs the way a business sells its products."

Political ads have several purposes. Some are used to help mold public opinion to mobilize either support or opposition with respect to a certain piece of legislation. Others are designed to convince voters to elect a particular

Bill Clinton shakes hands with construction workers during his 1992 presidential campaign. Because image is so important in political advertising, politicians try to market themselves to the common American voter.

political figure, or to prevent another from gaining office. Increasingly, political ads are employed to discredit those who do win elections and make it more difficult for them to govern.

These advertising approaches may satisfy the needs of those seeking power, but many critics wonder whether they are good for the democratic process. For one thing, thirty-second political commercials on TV or radio cannot possibly do justice to complex issues. Yet slogans are preferred to in-depth analysis in part because of the nature of advertising in the mass media. Not only are ads expensive, they also disappear quickly from the screen and must compete for recognition with thousands of other segments of broadcast material. That's why political advertisers believe they must use attention-getting techniques to entice viewers to watch or listen to the advertised message. Research has taught political advertisers to use brief images and quotes to get their message across as quickly as possible. Commonly called "sound bites," these short, catchy phrases tend to stick with voters longer than drawn-out substantive explanations. These sound bites are often vague in meaning, but they are popular with a large number of voters, each of whom can interpret the message to his or her liking. Helping Bill Clinton to victory in the 1992 presidential election, for example, was his sound bite, "I feel your pain."

But many political observers fear that political ads with all their gimmickry are increasingly taking the place of rational discussion of important issues. Some analysts even suggest that the simplification, partisanship, and negativity found in so many ads help to convince people to shun electoral politics altogether.

Despite these concerns, politicians continue to rely on modern advertising to win elections, or to stay in power.

The image or the message

Today one of the first acts of a candidate seeking high public office in the United States is to hire an advertising agency. With the ad agency's advice, candidates discover political strategies that largely bypass the task of winning debates against the opposition. Like their counterparts in the business world, experienced users of political ads know that the most effective promotions are those that appeal to emotions and feelings, not the intellect. As mass media expert Marshall McLuhan once said, "Politics and issues are useless for election purposes." Instead, as McLuhan was among the first to observe, the image of the candidate has become more important.

"Image" has several meanings in politics. At one level, it refers to how candidates look physically. The importance of appearance became abundantly clear in 1960 during the first-ever nationally televised debate between presidential candidates John F. Kennedy and Richard M. Nixon. Television, then still a fairly new mass medium, played a decisive role in determining the winner of the election. Kennedy's confident, youthful appearance, opposed to Nixon's visible perspiration, persuaded many television viewers to focus on the candidates' looks rather than their words. Polls at the time indicated that voters who listened to the debates on radio tended to think Nixon had won the verbal contest, while television viewers said Kennedy had argued better. Political consultants everywhere suddenly understood that a turning point in politics had been reached. From that moment on, deliberately created images became the lifeblood of politics in the United States.

Creating political images

Advertising agencies now specialize in helping candidates create the images that will sell well to the public. Cleverly applied makeup, favorable camera angles combined with dramatic soundtracks, attractive supporters,

In 1960, presidential candidates Richard M. Nixon (left) and John F. Kennedy (right) participated in the first nationally televised debate. This historic event was a turning point in both television and political advertising.

and inspiring locales enable advertisers to successfully "package" a candidate, developing for the office seeker the public image of a person who is patriotic, strong, intelligent, trustworthy, and caring.

But image has another meaning that goes beyond merely spruced-up appearance. Pictures, words, and sounds are used to define how a candidate is associated with certain political issues. Rather than supply details of a candidate's specific positions, however, political ads tend to generalize or stereotype, as all ads do. A candidate, for example, may decide to devise a public image of herself as an environmentalist. To do this, she can run ads that show her hiking in the mountains or visiting a famous environmental site that has been saved from destruction.

The "pseudo event"

To generate images quickly and dramatically, many political advertisers use what Pulitzer Prize–winning historian Daniel Boorstin calls a "pseudo event." On the surface, a pseudo event looks like a real and newsworthy happening, but it seldom is. Instead, it is usually a contrived occasion whose purpose is to provide a public forum for a candidate. At these staged events, amid much fanfare, the candidate gives a speech and makes himself available to TV photographers with the hope of appearing on the evening news. Although money must be spent to set up a pseudo event, the amount is invariably far less than the cost of producing a TV commercial and paying to have it aired.

Often the setting of a made-for-TV appearance creates a powerful and lasting impression with the public. Thus, candidates may have themselves photographed while shaking hands with assembly line workers at a car factory, visiting a shelter for the homeless, or conversing with powerful leaders of corporations. Republican presidential candidate George Bush once visited a flag factory to emphasize his patriotism. That night on the evening news he was portrayed smiling broadly against a sea of waving American flags—a useful and powerful image for any U.S. politician.

Presidential candidate Pat Buchanan is surrounded by throngs of supporters and cameramen during a visit to a lumber mill. Politicians often arrange staged events like this to get publicity and improve their political images.

Sometimes, though, advertisers' attempts to manipulate the media fail. In 1988, for example, pollsters told the Democratic presidential hopeful, Michael Dukakis, that rightly or wrongly, many voters perceived him as weak on matters of national defense. Knowing that this perception could hurt him at election time, the former Massachusetts governor visited a U.S. military installation and was photographed in the gun turret of a tank. Democratic strategists hoped this warrior image of the candidate would dispel any misgivings in the minds of voters. But the attempt largely failed. Even many supporters thought Dukakis, a small man, looked out of place, if not silly, in the tank. Somehow, the ad seemed inappropriate for him though it might have worked for a candidate of larger physical stature. Unfortunately for Dukakis, the ad mostly invited criticism, and reinforced the idea that he was not suitable as a military leader.

Going negative

Political advertisers often try to do more than make their clients look good. They also use negative advertising to make opponents look bad. In the world of business, negative advertising generally consists of unflattering statements about competing companies, brands, or products. The same concept is employed in politics. Whether it is aimed at political opponents' ideas, their reputations, or even their spouses and families, the purpose of a negative ad is to discredit or defame.

Some negative ads are seemingly mild. No matter how informational they purport to be, though, their intent is to

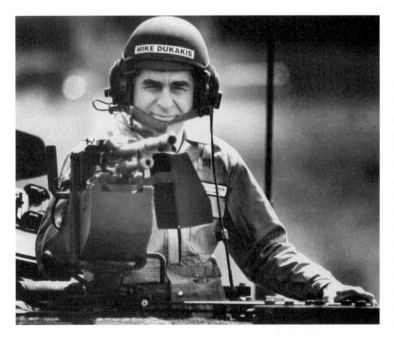

Presidential hopeful Michael Dukakis was photographed in the gun turret of a tank during his 1988 campaign. Dukakis hoped these publicity shots would enhance the public's opinion of his military abilities; however, the ads backfired when both supporters and opponents perceived the politician as small and awkward.

leave voters with an unfavorable impression. Such was the case during the early phase of the Clinton presidency. In 1992 opinion polls revealed a widespread consensus that federal action was needed to curb the rising cost of medical care. To address this problem, the new administration proposed a complex and highly controversial health care plan that would have constituted a major overhaul of the delivery and financing of medical care in this country.

Opposition developed immediately. Some of the plan's foes took to the airwaves with what became known as the "Harry and Louise" TV ads, which featured actors portraying a "yuppie" couple who worried that calamities awaited them if the administration's health care proposals became law. For example, the characters feared that they would be forced to change doctors. Although critics say that the Harry and Louise ads were often misleading, public support for the Democratic health care reform was measurably weaker within weeks of the ads' appearance.

Clinton supporters fought back with ads of their own. One target was the Pizza Hut Corporation, an outspoken opponent of the Clinton plan. The ad charged that the company didn't offer its employees proper health benefits. Four Washington, D.C.-area TV stations, however, declined to air the ad, and the controversy sparked a debate over free speech.

In the end, the anti-Clinton forces won the battle for public opinion. As a result of public pressure, the president's health care ideas were never officially debated by lawmakers. The fight had been costly: A total of $50 million was spent by all parties on advertising.

Attack ads

An extreme type of negative advertising is the "attack ad." Its purpose is to mount an open and direct personal assault on the opposition. An attack ad may claim that an opponent is dishonest, disloyal, or deceitful. "The aim of this new blood sport is to destroy a political agenda by tearing down the proponent's integrity," observes Owen Ullman of *Business Week.*

Not all attack ads focus on character defects. Some attempt to link an opponent with situations sure to arouse fear or indignation among a targeted segment of voters. This tactic was featured in a TV commercial supporting the 1992 reelection bid of Senator Jesse Helms of North Carolina. The image used in the video portion consisted of a white man's hands, shown crumpling a rejection letter; the voiceover commentary stated that the job in question had gone to a black person to fill a quota. Thus it was implied that Helms's opponent, Harvey Gantt, was an unconditional backer of affirmative action. Understandably, people all over the country complained loudly that the ad was a racist ploy, meant to pit white voters against black, but Helms won the election.

Deliberately provoking controversy

In fact, the controversy over the ad may have helped Helms. Commercial advertisers usually dread and avoid controversy; but those who use negative ads welcome it, often creating such promotional vehicles with the goal of provoking controversy. Advertisers have learned that a widely reported dispute over an ad will often generate free publicity for their clients when analysts and commentators discuss the issue in the mass media. Researchers have even determined that time given to this type of free coverage often exceeds that of paid ads. "Harry and Louise would just have been two more whiny yuppies had the media not taken up their lament," writes Gloria Borger of *U.S. News & World Report.*

However, purposefully courting controversy can also backfire. In October 1995, the Canadian Progressive Conservative Party ran personal attack ads against Jean Chretien, a leader of an opposition party. In the first ad, according to Canadian journalist Anthony Wilson Smith,

> the announcer asked: "Is this a prime minister?" The question was accompanied by unflattering photographs of Liberal leader Jean Chretien that would have been eliminated from a family album: eyes closed, dazed looks, close-up of his contorted mouth—the result of a birth defect.

A full-page newspaper advertisement attacks presidential candidate Steve Forbes's views on abortion.

The ad campaign ignited a storm of protest from Canadians of all political persuasions who abhorred the ads as distasteful and unfair. And when Canadian television newscasts replayed the ads plus reports of the controversy, public opinion mounted against the Progressive Conservatives, who finally saw no choice but to stop running the ads.

A growth industry?

Poll after poll reveals that most voters dislike negative ads. Ironically, though, surveys also indicate that a majority of people admit to being influenced by them. Says Roger Stone, a one-time Republican consultant: "Voters will tell you in focus groups that they don't like negative ads, but they retain the information so much better than the positive ones. The point is: people like dirty laundry. Why do tabloids sell?"

In fact, despite widespread condemnation, the use of negative advertising is gaining ground. *Newsweek* writer Jonathan Alter explains: "If millions were invested in TV ads arguing that a certain toothpaste rotted your teeth, would you buy that brand? Going negative works."

Demand for negative advertising is so great that it has sparked new opportunities for employment. "With television politics and campaigns hinging more and more on the personal peccadilloes of candidates, the need for fresh dirt has spawned a cottage industry, the professional life-ruiners," writes Ruth Shalit in the *New Republic*. Firms such as San Francisco–based Smart Campaigns and West Virginia–based Cunningham, Plante & Associates specialize in "opposition research," the first step in smearing a client's political opponents. These so-called oppo firms also offer to do "vulnerability studies" on their own clients to highlight weaknesses before opponents discover them. With negative ads becoming the norm in politics, many advertisers believe opposition research is a growth industry. One estimate holds that office seekers already spend $16 million for opposition research each year.

Not all support for negative advertising is based on the fact that it works. Some political consultants argue that such harsh tactics are needed to offset the self-serving and often misleading positive ads that candidates run about themselves. They point out that if negative information is true, voters have a right to hear it. Another argument suggests that negative advertising may give the election process a much-needed energy boost. "If it does nothing more than heighten attention to a campaign and increase voter turnout it's served a valuable purpose," says Robert Hinton, a one-time media director of the Tuesday Team ad agency. Not all industry observers, however, agree with this analysis.

Bad for democracy?

Voter turnout in the United States in recent years has been among the lowest of all modern democracies. And negative advertising may be partly responsible for this unenviable statistic. "One reason for the public's steadily deepening disdain for government is the increasing reliance by politicians on negative advertisements of an increasingly scabrous sort," suggests syndicated political columnist George Will.

And journalist Bill Moyers argues that negative advertising "is wrecking the [political organization] of America, destroying our ability as a cooperative society to face reality and solve our problems."

Whereas commercial advertising is subject to regulation if false claims are detected, no truth-in-campaigning laws exist for political speech. Political advertisers are free to say virtually anything without government interference. This almost unbridled liberty allows negative advertising to flourish in the United States.

Critics don't stop at negative ads, though. They complain about other aspects of political advertising, such as the growing tendency of politicians to rely on marketing research techniques developed in the business world to find out the latest trends in public opinion. According to this argument, political figures too often become slaves to such polls and temporary supporters of current fads, instead of leaders. They may be telling voters what they think people want to hear rather than what objective study indicates they need to hear. One party's candidates, for instance, may conclude from polls and focus groups that voters favor the idea of putting more criminals behind bars but don't want to hear about the new taxes that would be needed to pay for additional prisons. In response, these candidates may run ads featuring themselves as both tough on crime and in favor of tax cuts. What voters don't hear is discussion of exactly how new prisons can be built and paid for. Thus the other party may choose to run ads pointing this out and accusing the opposition of trying to have it both ways.

The cost of campaigning

The high cost of advertising produces yet another challenge to democracy. The Committee for the Study of the American Electorate estimated the cost of advertising a candidacy for the U.S. Senate in 1992 was about $2.4 million, while contenders for the House of Representatives had to pay an average of $250,000. The total amount spent

on advertising by all who sought seats in the Congress that year was $300 million. It was expected that by the end of 1996, this figure would top $500 million. TV advertising commands the lion's share of all these expenditures.

With this high price tag, people of modest means may no longer be able to run for national office. Few Americans have the resources to compete with candidates like magazine publisher Steve Forbes, who spent $30 million of his own money in an unsuccessful bid to become the 1996 presidential nominee of the Republican Party. Similarly, billionaire Ross Perot personally financed his own presidential campaign in 1992 and easily won the Reform Party's 1996 nomination over challenger Dick Lamm, a former governor of Colorado.

Many Americans across the political spectrum agree that stringent laws are needed to control how political

Because of the high cost of advertising, many people are unable to run for office. Businessman Steve Forbes (right) spent $30 million of his own money in a failed attempt to become the Republican Party's 1996 presidential nominee.

advertising is used. One idea advanced by the citizens group Common Cause is to reduce candidates' need for huge amounts of money by implementing campaign spending limits. In return, the government would provide matching funds for the advertising expenses of qualified candidates.

Other reformers suggest that the government could require broadcasters to give candidates free and equal amounts of time at no charge, on television, cable, radio, the Internet, and elsewhere. Congress could also enact tax breaks for broadcasters who offer candidates free time.

Another argument calls for changes in how advertising is bought on television. "Wouldn't it be a good idea for the FCC to give candidates a clear right to buy time in longer blocks than the much maligned 30-second ads?" asks Reed Hundt, chairman of the Federal Communications Commission. "Shouldn't we write rules that give broadcasters a real incentive to grant candidates' requests to buy, say, 5-minute blocks?" Hundt also offers a proposal for cheaper TV ad rates for candidates.

Many disagree with these ideas. Some politicians, in fact, think that *more* money should be spent on political advertising. To these advocates, an increase in advertising would guarantee a greater flow of information that helps voters make better decisions.

Political reformers think democracy is too important to be trusted to voters informed principally by paid advertisements. Propaganda, half-truths, and blatant lies that are too often disseminated by political advertising hardly substitute for honest debate and substantive discussion of the issues. Only reform, these critics insist, can curb electioneering abuses.

Whether any reforms will take place remains to be seen. One thing, though, is clear: Politics and advertising in America have become inseparable. As author James B. Twitchell puts it: "The culture we live in is carried on the back of advertising—literally. If you cannot find commercial support for what you have to say, it will not be transported."

Thus, advertising allows candidates and everyone else to join an increasing crowd of people who have something to say—and to sell.

6

Advertising and the Issue of Free Speech

MUCH OF THE ongoing dispute between advertisers and their critics centers on the issue of freedom of speech. This aspect of American life is so important that the founders of the country enshrined it in the Constitution. The First Amendment specifies that "Congress shall make no law . . . abridging the freedom of speech, or of the press."

This liberty does have limitations. For example, there are laws against slander and libel. In fact, many scholars believe that the framers of the Constitution originally intended the First Amendment to protect only political speech. Basically, this interpretation supports the right to voice an opinion on a political issue without having to worry about interference or punishment from the government.

During the nation's history, however, federal courts have ruled that literary and artistic forms of speech also deserve constitutional protection. But until the twentieth century there was little discussion in the courts about a form of expression not specifically mentioned in the constitution: commercial speech—especially the kind used in ads and commercials.

In recent decades, Americans have argued strenuously over whether advertisers have a constitutional right to publish, broadcast, or otherwise use commercial speech without government regulation. On one side of the debate are those who see nothing wrong with advertisers enjoying such protection as long as what they say is truthful and imparts information about a product that can legally be sold. A free flow of information, they say, is indispensable to consumers for making sound decisions in the marketplace. "No government—state, local or federal—has an open, unquestioned license to censor truthful commercial speech," declared a 1995 editorial from *Advertising Age*.

Opponents of this broad viewpoint respond that commercial speech is not a precious form of expression that reflects personal conviction. Nor is it essential to the flow of ideas needed to sustain a democracy or to achieve artistic expression. Rather, it is merely the language of salesmanship used to earn a profit. To raise commercial speech to a higher level of importance and give it full constitutional protection would trivialize educational, political, and artistic speech. In addition, a commonly held argument asserts, the government should have the authority to restrict commercial speech when the state has a strong interest in doing so; protecting the public health is cited as one legitimate source of strong state interest.

In New York City, a billboard for a local newspaper hawks "free speech, only a quarter," putting a price on the First Amendment equal to the price of its publication.

A billboard for Marlboro cigarettes depicts the company's well-known cowboy. Although opponents are trying to restrict the promotion of tobacco products, industry officials assert that their products are legal and should be granted freedom of speech.

By the mid-1990s, many debates swirled about the issue of commercial speech, but few could better illustrate the main controversy than the dispute over the advertising of tobacco products.

Do Tobacco advertisers have First Amendment rights?

Tobacco industry executives believe that smokers make up a market important and lucrative enough to justify advertising expenditures of over $6 billion each year.

Pitted against this industry effort are an array of health organizations, along with the federal government and several state governments, that repeatedly argue that smoking contributes to over three hundred thousand deaths a year. How, they wonder, can any society be aware that a product is so dangerous and yet allow its manufacturers to advertise for new customers? "Tobacco is the only consumer product that when used precisely as intended by its manufacturers kills about one-third of its users," notes Cliff Douglas, a one-time spokesman for an antismoking organization called the Coalition for Smoking or Health.

On January 11, 1979, U.S. surgeon general Julius B. Richmond called cigarette smoking "the single most important environmental factor contributing to early death." Since then, the federal government has taken several steps to curb smoking. Congress banned this activity on domestic commercial flights and in public buildings and imposed restrictions on cigarette advertising. In addition, the government began to require warning labels on cigarette products, advising consumers of possible risks associated with smoking.

Restricting commercial speech

Today, some organizations want further action. The American Medical Association, for example, urges a complete ban on the advertising of tobacco products. Though not willing to go that far, President Clinton in 1995 instructed the Food and Drug Administration to draft a series of aggressive regulations to keep tobacco away from teenagers.

The tobacco industry has fought all these restrictions and challenges in court and in public forums. It consistently argues that since its products are legal, there is no legal justification for restricting their promotion through advertising. Since tobacco companies are bound by the same truth-in-advertising laws that apply to other corporations, it can be said that safeguards against advertising abuse are already in place. Whether they function as designed in all cases is open to question.

As the tobacco industry and its opponents wrangle, similar battles over commercial free speech are in progress elsewhere in the business world. For example, many anti-alcohol groups believe that the advertising of alcoholic beverages should be restricted or eliminated. Meanwhile, other organizations seek similar restrictions on ads they don't like, irrespective of the nature of the product. The offending advertisements range from those that are said to be too sexually explicit to those that offend various ethnic, racial, religious, and political groups.

Yet, a common question underscores all the complaints: Do advertisers have a right to commercial speech? As always, Americans have turned to the courts to settle these disputes. But finding an answer there that satisfies every-one has proven difficult.

An uncertain legal struggle

The status of commercial speech remains unclear be-cause the courts have been inconsistent in their attempts to decide on whether governments can restrict advertising. "For most of the history of the republic, commercial speech received no legal protection whatsoever," says professor Steven H. Shiffrin, of Cornell University Law School.

This traditional legal position was ratified in the 1942 U.S. Supreme Court ruling in the case of *Valentine v. Chrestensen*, which concerned the legality of passing out advertising handbills. Commercial speech, said the Court, is different from other forms and is not necessarily pro-tected by the First Amendment.

Decades later, the Supreme Court upheld a 1971 con-gressional ban on the advertising of cigarettes on radio

and television. Unlike print media publishers, broadcasters are licensed by the government to use public airwaves and are subject to regulation by the FCC. Therefore, ruled the Court, the government also can regulate TV and radio advertising. Bans on TV and radio ads, however, do not apply to the advertising of the same products in other media such as billboards and magazines.

The prospect of giving the government authority to ban any broadcast advertising continues to worry many advertisers. If the government can censor advertising of certain products, such as cigarettes, on the grounds that associated activities, such as smoking, might be injurious to the public, what will be next? "One day Congress may use the same reasoning to outlaw the advertising of hand guns or of Toyotas," argues New Orleans attorney and free speech advocate Michael William Tifft. "Such bans would reach the newspapers, magazines, billboards, matchbox covers, flyers, who knows—perhaps word-of-mouth promotion." To date, such worries have been largely unfounded.

Commercial speech remained a less-protected form of speech when the Supreme Court softened its stance in 1975 with the case of *Bigelow v. Virginia*. At issue was the

Although cigarette advertising on television and radio was banned by the FCC in 1971, manufacturers can legally promote their products in other media, including billboards and magazines.

A billboard in Philadelphia advertises legal abortions in New York City. In a 1975 Supreme Court case, the Court ruled that abortion ads are protected by the First Amendment when they convey factual information, even though they are displayed in states where abortion is illegal.

advertising in Virginia—where abortion was illegal when the case began its journey through the judicial system—of the availability of abortions in New York—a state that permitted abortion. In the Court's opinion, the ads were a permissible means of transmitting factual information, and the state of Virginia had no authority to stop them.

Advertising victories and setbacks

Even more favorable decisions for advertisers followed. First, the Supreme Court knocked down a ban on the advertising of pharmaceutical drugs; next it overturned laws that had kept attorneys from advertising. In these and other similar cases the Court increasingly extended to commercial speech—as long as it was not false and deceptive—more, though not yet total, First Amendment protection.

In 1986, however, advertisers seemingly suffered a setback when the Supreme Court upheld a Puerto Rican law that banned the advertising of gambling in Puerto Rico, which is a U.S. commonwealth under the overall jurisdiction of the federal government. Since the government was not prevented from declaring gambling illegal, argued a majority of the justices, it could regulate the advertising of that activity.

By 1993, the Supreme Court had handed down several more decisions, but because they were so diverse, legal observers found it hard to identify a distinctive trend. On one hand, for example, the Court ruled that the federal government could restrict radio broadcast commercials for lotteries into neighboring states that forbid lotteries. But in 1993 the Court overturned a Cincinnati ban on commercial pamphlets placed on news racks normally devoted to magazines and newspapers, though Justice John Paul Stevens wrote in the majority opinion that this decision did not give commercial speech the same protection traditionally granted to political speech.

"Commercial speech still lacks the protection afforded political speech, but it is suddenly clear that [commercial speech] is covered by the First Amendment," observed Daniel Seligman of *Fortune* magazine following publication of the news rack ruling.

Three years later the Supreme Court issued what may be a landmark decision when it overturned a Rhode Island law that forbade the advertising of prices on alcoholic products in the hope that the lack of pricing would curb alcohol consumption. Nothing in the Constitution, the Court unanimously ruled, allows a state to restrict advertising of products that, though possibly dangerous, are nonetheless legal: "The 1st Amendment directs us to be especially skeptical of regulations that seek to keep people in the dark for what the government perceives to be their own good," wrote Justice Stevens.

A "substantial" interest

Some observers note that now the court system has adopted a legal standard to judge commercial speech cases. This standard requires that the government prove to a court's satisfaction that it has a "substantial" interest in blocking a specific advertisement. Defining a "substantial" interest is left to the court's discretion but it is less demanding than a "compelling" interest—that which the government must show in cases that demand a higher level of scrutiny.

No matter what adjectives judges use in their decision-making process, they have not ruled conclusively on the status of commercial speech. Until they do, Americans will continue to grapple over what advertisers can say. But there is another matter in any discussion of free speech that divides Americans. And it has to do with *where* commercial speech appears. Nothing illustrates this problem better than the debate to restrain outdoor advertising.

Billboards: blight or free speech?

The controversy over billboards has long been connected with the issue of commercial free speech. Some critics believe the more than half a million signs that now line the nation's highways and streets are safety hazards because they constantly divert drivers' attention from traffic. Others view them as "highway blight" and "visual pollution." Advertisers, however, believe it is their right to advertise on media such as billboards that are erected on privately owned or rented property.

A highway billboard beckons weary travelers to a Little America resort. Whether billboards are lining a highway or mounted on a building, they are effective advertising tools because their size and location make them hard to ignore.

What makes outdoor advertising unique is that unlike most other promotional messages, billboards can't be easily ignored. Writes William Ecenbarger in the *Seattle Times/Post-Intelligencer,*

The billboard is advertising's slam dunk. You can't turn the page, you can't change the station. The junk mail of the American highway. It intrudes on our view, blocking mountains, coastlines and skylines. Billboard companies are selling something they don't own—our range of vision, no one has been able to stop them.

Regardless of the free speech controversy surrounding billboards, many consumers enjoy reading the ads— especially tourists looking for places to visit.

Through the years, billboards have so incensed people that many have tried to tax them into nonexistence or ban them altogether. Some protesters have chopped them down, which of course is against the law, since the billboards themselves are private property.

Billboards provide many benefits, however. They are especially useful in a state like Florida that receives over forty million tourists each year. Many motorists along interstates are pleased to see road signs telling them where to exit for their favorite restaurants, service stations, and motels. Some even say that reading billboards helps them pass the time more quickly, or prevents accidents by keeping weary drivers awake. All these reasons help enforce the free speech argument that a free flow of information enables consumers to make decisions for themselves.

But does consumers' need for information mean that any restriction placed on outdoor advertising automatically constitutes an attack on free speech? After all, for decades courts have ruled that even political free speech can be regulated by governments in terms of "time and place." For example, a political candidate who sets up a loud amplifier in a suburban neighborhood and broadcasts a campaign speech at 2:00 A.M. would get people's attention but might also be violating local laws that uphold quiet hours. But the candidate could most likely make the same speech, similarly amplified, during daylight hours at a public park.

Billboard restrictions and bans

Persuaded by such arguments, several communities across the country have passed ordinances restricting the size of billboards and banning them completely from certain locations. Some states, including Hawaii, Alaska, Maine, and New Mexico, have banned them entirely along all state, county, and municipal roads.

Such efforts don't always succeed, however. Opposition from the Outdoor Advertising Association of America (OAAA), with the support of an array of advertising firms, campground owners, and retailers, often suffices to stop attempts to bring down the signs. Though the economic self-interest of the business groups is clear, they tend to present their objections to proposed bans on outdoor advertising in terms such as "infringement on free speech."

Congress tried to reduce so-called highway blight when it passed the Highway Beautification Act of 1965 to eliminate billboards from interstate highways, which are federally funded and come under the jurisdiction of the U.S. Department of Transportation. Though many signs came down, the legislation never accomplished what its backers intended. Instead, outdoor advertisers found loopholes in the law that allowed them to put up new signs. The OAAA later persuaded Congress to amend the act to require that billboard companies receive government compensation for their losses. Today, however, a financially strapped Congress lacks enough funds to reimburse all billboard owners. So, the interstate highways remain cluttered with signs.

Elsewhere, away from major expressways, another battle over billboards is being waged. This time government officials are concerned over *who* is being targeted by advertising. In 1995, for example, the Baltimore City Council prohibited the posting of outdoor liquor and tobacco ads in its inner city. The council believed that advertisers were deliberately targeting minority youth living in the downtown area. To protect these young citizens, who were considered to be very susceptible to advertising, the city banned the ads.

But the city's action prompted a lawsuit from the Anheuser-Busch beer company and Penn Advertising, which want the ban revoked. Free speech, say the plaintiffs, is the issue. In addition, the Association of National Advertisers and the American Association of Advertising Agencies filed a legal brief arguing: "If lawful speech directed to adults can be censored merely because it is said to promote the wrong attitude in teenagers, almost no controversial speech is safe from government control."

Nonetheless, many parents, educators, and child advocates believe that some ads for products such as alcohol and tobacco are directed toward the youth market. They insist that children deserve special protection from billboards and other public advertisement displays that they feel are clearly targeting an underage audience.

Those who favor restrictions on advertising aimed at youth often advance the argument that if the government

A billboard advertising Newport cigarettes hangs on the graffiti-covered wall of a New York bodega. Efforts to ban tobacco and alcohol ads in economically depressed areas have led to lawsuits over the issue of free speech.

has an interest in protecting all citizens from the hazards of addictive substances and gambling, there is, by extension, an obligation to offer special protection to children, who are perhaps the most vulnerable to advertising's allure.

This suggestion, however, is opposed by advertisers, who invoke the First Amendment. In addition, many businesspeople express the concern that if government were allowed to regulate any type of advertising for the purpose of protecting children, the door would be open to further restrictions.

This division of opinion becomes even more apparent when the focus is on television—the medium that plays the biggest role in conveying advertisers' messages to children.

But TV hasn't always been a primary force in advertising. During the early days of television, many thinkers predicted that the new medium would one day enrich human lives with programs dedicated to the arts and high culture. Instead, television developed into a medium driven by commercial advertising's need to sell things. Broadcasters, of course, must have advertisers to assure their existence. But except for PBS, C-Span, and a few other cable stations, the broadcast industry's chief mission is to make a profit—and the money comes from advertising dollars.

The role of broadcast media

Broadcast media are so important to the discussion of commercial free speech because the nation's airwaves are owned by the general public, not by individuals. These airwaves are managed by the federal government. For this reason, those wanting to do business via the national frequencies must be licensed and must agree to accept government regulation.

Anyone can publish a newspaper or magazine and exercise almost unlimited freedom of speech. Moreover, the government does not restrict the number of ads in periodicals. Yet, for years, the same standards did not apply to the broadcast industry. The FCC required broadcasters to serve the "public interest" if they wanted a license to operate. This meant that, among other things, TV advertisers

had to limit the advertising aimed at children with respect to both kind and frequency.

In the early 1980s, however, officials at the FCC believed that too many rules and regulations intruded on broadcasters' First Amendment rights. Accordingly, the FCC abolished many broadcasting restrictions, including those that had limited the length, content, and number of commercials that targeted children.

As a result, prime time for children's programs was "quickly overrun by toy and food companies eager to create programs that featured their products. News, educational programs and other types of TV broadcasting for children virtually disappeared, replaced by programs that commanded higher advertising rates," say authors Minow and LaMay in *Abandoned in the Wasteland: Children, Television and the First Amendment.*

Eventually, though, the public balked at giving broadcasters such a free hand at selling to the nation's youth, and in the 1990s Congress passed the Children's Television Act and restored some time limits on commercials aimed at kids. The act also requires broadcasters to offer more educational programming for the young and to run these presentations during the morning and afternoon when children are likely to be watching.

The National Association of Broadcasters (NAB) opposes the new requirements. Doug Wills, the group's spokesman, says: "Those issues [imposed commercial time limits and educational programming quotas] are non-negotiable. The bottom line for us is a First Amendment concern."

Anything goes?

As commercial speech inches toward increased constitutional protection, American society continues to witness a great change in the standards of advertising. Many ads common today were once forbidden by either government regulation or public opinion. Not long ago, for instance, manufacturers and stores could not air TV ads showing women's undergarments. Today, though, commercials and ads routinely feature young women in lingerie.

Even more controversial were Calvin Klein's advertisements in which young models of both sexes were photographed in sexually evocative poses to promote the designer's line of clothes. *Advertising Age* describes one of Klein's 116-page magazine ads as "the most striking example of a vast range of jeans, lingerie and cosmetics ads that once would have been relegated to *Playboy* or *Penthouse* but now are appearing in upscale mainstream publications." Critics have demanded that criminal charges of child pornography be pressed against Klein because of some of his recent ads, but the company withdrew the offending ads and the matter was dropped. Controversy over the ads, meanwhile, helped sell the products.

Television now teems with commercials featuring laxatives, sanitary pads, antiyeast creams, deodorants, and condoms that once could not be mentioned on the airwaves.

Even words once considered taboo—words that sometimes led to arrest for violation of local decency codes—now appear in advertising. One ad maker told journalist R. Lee Sullivan that his firm uses "uncouth language on the grounds that good ads mirror the speech of the audience they're meant to reach. If people are sprinkling more four-letter words into their conversations, copywriters should feel free to use them in ads."

To many observers, the highly expressive language found in some ads merely reflects changes in American society. "Advertising standards have always been defined by the public's tolerance and the shifting moods of courts and government agencies," writes journalist Thomas Easton.

Even so, many Americans are offended by much of the advertising they see and hear presented under the mantle of commercial speech. Industry critics believe that many ads do great damage to the moral fabric of society.

But is the solution to restrict the advertising industry?

Many think so. They'd like to see the FCC impose stricter guidelines on television and radio advertising. A few groups favor bans of one type or another. Some health organizations, for example, want to put an end to "junk

Controversy over Calvin Klein's clothing ads helped to sell his line, despite critics' charges that the ads were a form of child pornography.

food" commercials on children's programs. And the non-profit Center for the Study of Commercialism, in Washington, D.C., is seeking an end to product placement promotions in feature films.

Yet other Americans, including some critics of advertising, resist the call to impose new restrictions of any sort on the industry, which may be already one of the most highly regulated commercial arenas in the nation. Instead, many of these critics exhibit their displeasure with advertising in other ways. Every year, for instance, Women Against Pornography bestows an award—a plastic pig—to advertisers whose work offended the group. And *Consumer Reports* regularly publishes articles that criticize the advertising industry for activities that allegedly prey on children. Other organizations launch boycotts against advertisers they don't like or produce ads of their own to rebut commercial speech they disagree with.

A protester boycotts the Philip Morris Company, a giant in the tobacco industry. Like any form of free speech, advertising is subject to the public's approval or disapproval.

Free speech of any type always invites criticism, and perhaps threats of boycotts, when it enters the marketplace of ideas. Up to a point, the public forum provides its own self-governing mechanism. Popular opinion can sometimes abolish bad or unpopular ideas faster than any government ban.

That's why some people think commercial speech is simply another form of communication that should be

freely expressed, and then subjected to the forces of public approval or disapproval. If a promotion offends too many consumers, the advertiser can expect to lose money and will presumably drop the ad. The government, say advocates of commercial free speech, has no business dictating what advertisers can or cannot say. Freedom of speech means precisely that: the liberty to say what one wants, whether it's an opinion about whom to vote for—or an urgent message telling people what to buy.

But this claim may be overused. Television, after all, isn't just a domain for the debating of ideas. It is owned, or controlled, by wealthy corporate advertisers who wield much more power than is affordable by, or accessible to, individual consumers. Many advertisers turn almost reverentially to the U.S. Constitution to ward off any attempts to modify or ban their ads. Predictably, then, the debate focuses on the First Amendment rather than, say, whether the TV advertisements of a toy gun manufacturer incite violent behavior among children.

So often is freedom of speech used to justify the sale of virtually anything on the market that many consumers are left confused. Those who complain about the propriety of TV commercials often find themselves accused of advocating censorship, when they really were suggesting that advertisers should govern themselves. Authors Minow and LaMay observe: "Apparently [the United States is] a country in which a television set is a device whose only purpose is to sell things, and where anything that impedes that goal—even self-regulation—is said to violate the First Amendment."

Often quoted in debates concerning the First Amendment are the words of Voltaire, the famous eighteenth-century French playwright, philosopher, and champion of free political speech: "I detest what you write, but I would give my life to make it possible for you to continue to write." Many wonder if today's commercial speech could command such a spirited defense.

Suggestions for Further Reading

Kathlyn Gay, *Caution! This May Be an Advertisement.* New York: Franklin Watts, 1992. This book, aimed at young adults, presents a highly readable and comprehensive examination of advertising.

Charles A. Goorum and Helen Dalrymple, *Advertising in America: The First 200 Years.* New York: Harry N. Abrams, 1990. A colorfully illustrated and entertaining history of advertising for the general reader.

Scholastic Update, May 7, 1993. This entire issue, written for teens, explores many aspects of the social issues surrounding advertising.

Anne E. Weiss, *The School on Madison Avenue, Advertising and What It Teaches.* New York: E. P. Dutton, 1980. This very readable work includes historical information and an explanation of tricks of the advertising trade and the impact of the industry on social issues in America.

Works Consulted

Scott Adams, "Targeting to Ethnic Groups Is Becoming More Popular," *University of Florida News*. Gainesville, January 12, 1996.

Jonathan Alter, "The Mad Doctrine of Politics," *Newsweek*, November 7, 1994.

American Voices: Prize-Winning Essays on Freedom of Speech, Censorship and Advertising Bans. New York: Philip Morris, 1987.

Deborah Baldwin, "Read This," *Common Cause*, May/June 1991.

Dudley Barlow, "Sands Wouldn't Do It," *Education Digest*, May 1992.

Michael Barone, "Anatomy of a Victory," *U.S. News & World Report*, March 18, 1996.

Kimberly Blanton, "Amid the Uproar, Sex Still Sells," *Boston Globe*, October 18, 1991.

Gloria Borger, "Stupid Advertising Tricks," *U.S. News & World Report*, August 1, 1994.

Gorton Carruth, *What Happened When: A Chronology of Life & Events in America.* New York: Signet, Penguin Books, 1991.

Charles Clark, "Advertising Under Attack, Part One and Part Two," *CQ Researcher*, September 13, 1991.

Eric Clark, *The Want Makers: The World of Advertising: How They Make You Buy.* New York: Viking-Penguin, 1988.

Michael Clements, "No-Smoking Battle Just Warming Up," *Detroit News*, February 25, 1990.

Steven Colford, "Big Win for Commercial Speech: Industry Cheers," *Advertising Age,* March 29, 1993.

———, "High Court Hits Commercial Speech Hard: Ruling in N.C. Lottery Case Strikes a Blow to Advertising Industry," *Advertising Age*, June 28, 1993.

"Deceptive Advertising," *Consumers' Research*, April 1994.

Warren Dunn (chairman and chief executive officer, Miller Brewing Company), "Government-Mandated Warnings on Alcohol Advertisements: Unnecessary, Ineffective, Harmful and Unconstitutional," *Vital Speeches of the Day*, July 15, 1993.

Alan Thein Durning, "Can't Live Without It," *World Watch,* May/June 1993.

Thomas Easton, "Does Sex Really Sell? Explicit Print, TV Ads Arouse Debate," *New York Bureau of the Baltimore Sun*, September 29, 1991.

William Ecenbarger, "The Billboard: Still King of the Road," *Seattle Times/Post-Intelligencer*, October 4, 1987.

Alice Embree, "Madison Avenue Brainwashing: The Facts," *In the Marketplace: Consumerism in America.* Edited by the editors of *Ramparts* with Frank Browning. San Francisco: Canfield Press, 1972.

Lionel Fisher, "Adverguising," *Oregonian*, August 9, 1992.

Alexandra Greeley, "Food Labels: Consumer Confusion," *The World & I*, January 1990.

S. C. Gwynne, "Hot News in Class," *Time*, December 18, 1995.

Joe Haberstroh, "The Color of Advertising," *Seattle Times*, October 28, 1990.

Debra Gersh Hernandez, "Ban on Billboard Alcohol Ads Is Challenged, Free Speech and Advertising Groups Say the City of Baltimore's Ban Is Unconstitutional," *Editor & Publisher*, July 16, 1994.

Cheryl Heuton, "FCC Again Defers Ruling on Kid Shows," *Adweek*, March 13, 1995.

Carole M. Howard, "Advertising and Public Relations: A Vital Partnership to Help Achieve Your Clients' Goals," *Vital Speeches of the Day,* November 17, 1993.

Reed Hundt, "Revitalizing Democracy in the Information Age," *Vital Speeches of the Day*, January 15, 1996.

Nikhil Hutheesing, "The Wild West of Advertising," *Forbes*, January 16, 1995.

Carla Koehl and Sarah Van Boven, with bureau reports, "Calling All Media Planners," *Newsweek*, August 24, 1995.

Barbara Lippert, "Map'ing the Territory," *Adweek*, July 3, 1995.

Nancy S. Maldonado, "Making TV Environmentally Safe for Children," *Childhood Education*, Summer 1992.

Maria Mallory, "That's One Angry Camel," *Business Week*, March 7, 1994.

Sean McCollum, "Nothing but the Truth?" *Scholastic Update*, May 7, 1993.

William McGowan, "Class Ads," *Scholastic Update*, May 7, 1993.

Newton N. Minow and Craig L. LaMay, *Abandoned in the Wasteland: Children, Television and the First Amendment.* New York: Hill and Wang, 1995.

Judy Monroe, "Alcohol and Ads: What Effect Do They Have on You?" *Current Health 2*, November 1994.

Judith E. Nichols, *By the Numbers*. Chicago: Bonus Books, 1990.

David Ogilvy, *Ogilvy on Advertising*. New York: Crown Publishers, 1983.

Vance Packard, *The Hidden Persuaders*. New York: David McKay, 1957.

Karen N. Peart, "At Odds with the Ads," *Scholastic Update*, May 7, 1993.

Anne G. Perkins, "The Costs of Deception," *Harvard Business Review*, May/June 1994.

"Quackery Targets Teens," *FDA Consumer*, February 1988.

O. Lee Reed, "Should the First Amendment Protect Joe Camel? Toward an Understanding of Constitutional 'Expression,'" *American Business Law Journal*, February 19, 1995.

Leah Rickard and Jeanne Whalen, "Retail Trails Ethnic Changes," *Advertising Age*, May 1, 1995.

Joe Saltzman, "Infomercials—Television's Newest Success," *USA Today*, September 1994.

David Savage, "Advertisers' Free-Speech Rights Bolstered," *Los Angeles Times*, June 14, 1996.

George Seldes, *The Great Thoughts*. New York: Ballantine Books, 1985.

Daniel Seligman, "The Voice of Commerce," *Fortune*, May 31, 1993.

"Selling to School Kids," *Consumer Reports*, May 1995.

Ruth Shalit, "The Oppo Boom," *New Republic*, January 3, 1994.

Michael Shedlin, "Advertising: Its Life and Times," *People's Almanac*, Garden City, NY: Doubleday, 1975.

Eric Shine, "From the Folks Who Brought You Harry and Louise . . . ," *Business Week*, April 17, 1995.

Phil Sudo, "Ads All Around," *Scholastic Update*, May 7, 1993.

Lisa Sullivan, "Hails Attention to Disabled" (letter), *Advertising Age*, June 26, 1995.

R. Lee Sullivan, "Crude Doesn't Sell," *Forbes*, October 24, 1994.

Max Sutherland, *Advertising and the Mind of the Consumer: What Works, What Doesn't and Why*. St. Leonards, Australia: Allen & Unwin, 1993.

Ira Teinowitz, "Philip Morris Hits Youth Smoking," *Advertising Age*, July 10, 1995.

"The 30-Second Seduction: A *Consumer Reports* Special on Television Advertising" (video). Mount Vernon, NY: Consumer Reports TV, Consumers Union of the United States, 1985.

James B. Twitchell, "Advertising Carries Our Culture," *Orlando* (FL) *Sentinel*, June 2, 1996.

Owen Ullman, "The Politics of Poison: Have Personal Attacks Gone Too Far?" *Business Week*, March 27, 1995.

Betsy Wagner, "Our Class Is Brought to You Today by . . . ," *U.S. News & World Report*, April 24, 1995.

Ellen Wartella, "The Commercialization of Youth: Channel One in Context," *Phi Delta Kappan*, February 1995.

Stacey Welling, "Minorities Targeted as Consumers," *Las Vegas Review-Journal*, July 22, 1990.

"Why Does Ottawa Need to Advertise to Tell Us What a Superlative Job It's Doing?" *Alberta Report/Western Report*, September 25, 1995.

Ellen Willis, "Women and the Myth of Consumerism," *In the Marketplace: Consumerism in America*. Edited by the editors of *Ramparts* with Frank Browning. San Francisco: Canfield Press, 1972.

George Will, "Smoking Out the Tobacco Disaster," *Detroit News*, February 25, 1990.

Anthony Wilson-Smith, "Indecent Exposures," *Maclean's*, October 25, 1995.

Dave Winans, "Trash or Treasure?" *NEA Today*, March 1996.

Gail Baker Woods, *Advertising and Marketing to the New Majority: A Case Study Approach*. Belmont, CA: Wadsworth, 1995.

Index

About the Author

John Dunn is a freelance writer and high school history teacher. He has taught in Georgia, Florida, North Carolina, and Germany. As a writer and journalist, he has published over 250 articles and stories in more than 20 periodicals, as well as scripts for audiovisual productions and a children's play. His books—*The Russian Revolution, The Relocation of the North American Indian*, and *The Spread of Islam*—were published by Lucent Books. He lives with his wife and two daughters in Ocala, Florida.

Picture Credits